Religion in American Public Schools

By RICHARD B. DIERENFIELD

Associate Professor of Education,
Macalester College

FOREWORD BY BISHOP JAMES A. PIKE

Public Affairs Press, Washington, D.C.

TO MY WIFE AND MY PARENTS

FOREWORD

One of the most significant events in American constitutional history was the recent decision of the United States Supreme Court in *Engle v. Vitale.* While the holding itself was a narrow one—namely, that a State-authorized prayer may not be used in the public schools, even voluntarily as far as student participation is concerned—the logical implications of the decision as to the relationship of religion to public life are broad indeed. Few decisions in the history of the court have caused such widespread public discussion—indeed controversy.

It is fortunate that just at this time we are provided through Professor Dierenfield's exhaustive study a clear picture of what actually has been going on in public education throughout the country with reference to religious observances, activities and instruction. This provides the much needed factual base for the intelligent forming of opinions and corporate decision on the part of our citizens. It is particularly important in the light of the fact that forms of constitutional amendment have been introduced into Congress and that should Congress adopt any one of these proposed amendments, through the ratifying process in the States there will be widespread public consideration of this whole matter. The work is particularly valuable because of its objectivity. Whatever may be the view of a given reader on the various items of school-religion relationship here surveyed, he can at least ground his judgment on facts as to the historical and present extent of these given connections.

It is no secret that I do not agree with the Supreme Court's decision. Yet, on the other hand, I am certainly not prepared to support with enthusiasm all of the practices of schools as portrayed in this book; and some readers, I am sure, will approve of none. But all readers, I believe, will be surprised at the extent in which religion has played a part in our public schools. Though the author is not trying to "prove a point" either way, I feel that his description of actual practices endorses my position that the American tradition in regard to religion in public life has followed a "middle way" between church-State union, on the one hand, and secularization of public life on the other.

This study adds to our knowledge of the numerous instances where throughout our history we have followed the "middle way". I believe that it is as neutral as any way we will find: for example, the New York Regents' prayer, while certainly free of the assertion of the dogmatic

scheme of any particular group, and while certainly quite minimal in its
religious instruction aspects, does point to a reality beyond the nation
and beyond the subject-matter in the curriculum—which for pragmatic
reasons in a pluralistic society must be almost completely areligious.
Not to point *beyond* is not neutral because the total effect then is secularism—albeit by default rather than by intent; secularism itself is a
religion, i.e., a world-view taken on faith. And this is true of the many
other instances where, under the auspices of the State, prayers are said
and God is recognized—including everything from the prayers in Congress and the Supreme Court to "In God We Trust" on the coins, the
eye of Providence in the obverse of the Great Seal on dollar bills, and
"under God" in the Pledge of Allegiance.

It is my belief, as I had an opportunity to say in my testimony before
the Senate Judiciary Committee, that the forms of proposed amendment which would list exceptions to the First Amendment would be
unwise, and now with the material in this book I am all the more con-
vinced that to list the scores of instances which have been part of our
tradition would be a hopeless task. I feel rather that we should *affirm*
the First Amendment, restating the establishment clause in terms of
what the Founding Fathers were really trying to get at, in some such
words as "the recognition as an established church of any denomination, sect, or religious association." This would preserve the separation
of Church and State, whereas, e.g., in the New York prayer, no church
was actually involved; and certainly our Founding Fathers, and many
of us today would not desire the separation of religion from society.

But it is not my purpose here to elaborate the argument for my position; I state it in order to show how valuable this material is to those
who hold this position. But I believe the book will be equally interesting and valuable to those who support the Supreme Court's ruling and
would spread its logic to uproot all such practices. For them this
volume will provide a detailed blueprint for the task ahead; indeed
they will see the task of such magnitude that some may rethink their
position. But for those for which it will not, the book will be a valuable
guide as to a time-table for political and judicial action in this regard.
For all it will provide a better opportunity than we have ever had to
evaluate particular practices and possibilities in terms of the design of
what each will feel is the right solution in this very difficult field in our
happily heterogeneous common life.

JAMES A. PIKE

The Cathedral Close
San Francisco

PREFACE

The relationship between religion and public education in the United States is controversial and constantly changing. When public schools became popular during the first part of the 19th century, religion constituted an important influence in their operation. By the dawn of the 20th century, however, many aspects of religion had been eliminated either through strict adherence to Constitutional amendments or sectarian jealousy. Fears that the schools were becoming "Godless" did, however, encourage local boards and state legislatures to permit a wide variety of religious activities in public schools. The legality of a number of these activities in public schools has been tested in state and federal courts from time to time and the nature of permissible practice becomes clearer.

On June 25, 1962, the United States Supreme Court shed further light on the subject when it handed down a momentous ruling involving the use of a government written and sponsored prayer in the schools of New York. The suit was brought by Mr. Steven I. Engel, et al., against the Board of Education of Union Free School District No. 9 of New Hyde Park, New York. The disagreement centered about the following short prayer to be said aloud by each class at the beginning of every school day: "Almighty God, we acknowledge our dependence upon Thee, and we beg Thy blessings upon us, our parents, our teachers and our country." This procedure was recommended to the school systems of New York by the state board of regents which had composed the prayer. Children who did not wish to participate could either remain silent or be excused from the room when the prayer was said.

The respondents argued that no violation of the Constitution took place because the prayer was non-denominational in nature and that students were not forced to repeat the words. The New York Court of Appeals agreed with this logic and had declared the practice constitutional. The Supreme Court of the United States overturned the lower court in a 6-1 decision and ruled such prayer was a violation of the First and Fourteenth amendments. The following quotations from the majority opinion, written by Justice Black, illustrate the thinking of the Court:

"We think that by using its public school system to encourage recitation of the Regents' prayer, the State of New York has adopted a practice wholly inconsistent with the Establishment Clause."

"There can, of course, be no doubt that New York's program of daily classroom invocation of God's blessings as prescribed in the Regents' prayer is a religious activity."

"When the power, prestige and financial support of government is placed behind a particular religious belief, the indirect coercive pressure upon religious minorities to conform to the prevailing officially approved religion is plain."

"It is neither sacreligious nor antireligious to say that each separate government in this country should stay out of the business of writing or sanctioning official prayers and leave that purely religious function to the people themselves and to those the people choose to look to for religious guidance."

The immediate reaction to this decision ranged from the opinion of Cardinal Spellman who was "shocked and frightened" at a ruling which "strikes at the very heart of the Godly tradition in which America's children have for so long been raised" to Jewish and Unitarian groups favoring it.

Clergy opinion, both Protestant and Roman Catholic, appeared generally hostile to the decision, while public reaction reflected a strong concern over the implications of the Court's position. Upon reflection and closer examination of the ruling, however, a change has taken place in the attitude of many people. An important footnote which Justice Black inserted has allayed the fears of some that the intent was to do away with any and all religious references in public life:

"There is, of course, nothing in the decision that is inconsistent with the fact that school children and others are officially encouraged to express love for our country by reciting historical documents such as the Declaration of Independence which contain references to the Deity or by singing officially espoused anthems which include the composer's professions of faith in a Supreme Being, or with the fact that there are many manifestations in our public life of belief in God."

A comparison of the opinion written by Justice Black and the separate concuring opinion of Justice Douglas shows the relative mildness of the Black statement. Douglas advocated complete elimination of any religious practices financed by taxes. This would include chaplains for House and Senate and the use of any person who is on the public payroll to offer prayer at governmental gatherings.

The course of public opinion on the Court's attitude will doubtless undergo further modification in the months to come. Three significant cases will come up for review during the fall term of the Court. The Pennsylvania law requiring ten verses of the Bible to be read daily will reach the Supreme Court after twice being ruled unconstitutional by a federal district court in Philadelphia. In Maryland the state supreme court has upheld the legality of Bible reading as well as the recitation of the Lord's Prayer. This case also has been appealed to the U.S. Supreme Court. Another suit to be reviewed arises from a decision by the Florida supreme court which deals with use of religious ceremonies and songs in public schools. After decisions on these cases have been rendered, the legal status of several types of religious activities in public schools will be more clearly defined. Many legal rulings, much analysis and investigation together with experimentation and friendly cooperation by all groups concerned are necessary if progress is to be made toward resolving the issue.

The future position of religious influence in public schools is difficult to forsee because of the many variables involved. The serious nature of the issue makes necessary concentrated effort to find answers to questions which presently block a solution of the difficulty. This book is dedicated to the purpose of providing information to men of good will, thus assisting them to deal successfully with the problem of religion in public education.

RICHARD B. DIERENFIELD

Macalester College
St. Paul, Minnesota

CONTENTS

CHAPTER I

THE ISSUE

The issue of religion in tax supported schools is one of the most vexing problems facing American education today.

The heat from this controversy over religious influence in public schools blows sometimes warm, sometimes hot; but rarely cold. During the past several years, the fever pitch intensity of this issue in many parts of the country has provoked such headlines as:

"School Prayer Upheld in New York"[1]
"Religion Is Issue in North Dakota Schools"[2]
"Christmas Carols in School OK, Official Rules"[3]

This is indeed a "hot" issue—as the extensive involvement of both individuals and organizations indicates. Federal aid to public education flounders in protracted sectarian religious battles; national organizations of educators strive toward effective solutions; while powerful church bodies pass resolutions urging the schools to include more religious emphasis in their programs.

What strikes the reader of current literature on the subject is how much has been written about the philosophical aspects involved in any suggested solution. One assumes it is not a mistake to *begin* on the ideological and conceptual level, but unfortunately, up to the present time, much of the thinking *ends* there. An urgent need exists for more practical, definite, and usable information.

The results of a survey of American public school systems recently completed by the writer are included in this book to document the extent to which religious influence exists in public education. Questionnaires were sent to superintendents of school systems in 4,000 communities throughout all parts of the country. Of these, 54.57% replied, giving details on practices used in their own localities.[4] These figures, which have not been available until now will throw light on many aspects of the relationship between public schools and religion.

A brief analysis of some of the factors which make the problem both current and confusing may be helpful.

Following World War II, religion experienced a noticeable renaissance in the United States, a phenomenon called by some authorities a "revival," by others a "phony revival." However, theo-

1

logian Reinhold Neibuhr maintains that "no one can question the
fact that we are experiencing a marked increase of interest in religion
if not a revival of religious faith."[5] The present work does not pur-
port to inquire into the authenticity of this resurgence of religious
enthusiasm, but rather to collect some much-needed factual information about one of its manifestations.

Attention of Religious Bodies. The churches are concerned about
the handling of religion by the public schools. Nearly all major
denominations have issued statements expressing their concern about
religion in public schools, and defined their positions. Since it is
impossible to find one statement which will satisfy all the adherents
to even one denomination, the quotations presented below do not, of
course, represent unanimous agreement. They do, however, reflect
the majority opinion in the three main divisions of religious faith.

1. The Jewish position maintains that the public schools should
leave religion alone. There are some differences of opinions among
secular and religious leaders, but the following statement represents
the views of a large segment of the Jewish population:

"The maintenance and furtherance of religion are the responsibilities of the synagogue, the church, and the home, and not of the
public school system: the utilization in any manner of the time,
facilities, personnel, or funds of the public school system for purposes of
religious instruction should not be permitted."[6]

"We are opposed to governmental aid to schools under the super-
vision or control of any religious denomination or sect, whether Jewish,
Protestant, or Catholic, including outright subsidies, transportation,
textbooks, and other supplies."[7]

2. The Roman Catholic position, in general, holds that more
religion should be introduced into the public schools and that parochial school children should receive either "fringe benefits" or direct
grants from public tax money. Archbishop Hoban, President-General
of the National Catholic Education Association, states: "We must
appeal to American honesty and ingenuity to find a solution to the
problem of restoring religion to the curriculum of all schools without
injury to the rights of every child."[8]

The late Cardinal Stritch of Chicago has said: "We have no
hesitancy in saying that the exclusion of religious instruction from
public education is to be regretted and not praised as some kind of
a symbol of so-called democratic faith."[9]

3. The Protestant attitude cannot be completely expressed in

one statement, as each denomination places emphasis on somewhat different points; but there is general agreement on the need for additional stress on religious heritage, freedom of religion, and maintenance of the separation of church and state.

In its last official pronouncement on the subject, the General Board of the National Council of Churches took the following stand: "It is expected that they (the public schools) shall teach that religion is an essential aspect of our national heritage and culture, that this nation subsists under the governance of God and that our moral and ethical values rest upon religious grounds and sanctions." [10]

Individual church bodies take stronger positions because of homogeneity of belief. For instance, this policy was adopted by the General Conference of the Methodist Church: "We believe that religion has a rightful place in the public school program, and that it is possible for public school teachers, without violating the traditional American principle of separation of church and state, to teach moral and spiritual values. We hold that it is possible, within this same principle . . . to integrate religious instruction with the regular curriculum . . . " [11]

The role of religion in public education is made more complex by contradictory laws and court decisions. State codes vary greatly in the kind and amount of religious influence allowed in school systems under their jurisdiction. Rulings by both state and federal courts lack uniformity, and this creates disagreement on the legality of many practices.

An essential step in approaching any emotionally charged issue is to determine, as objectively as possible, the situation as it actually exists. With this aim in mind, present custom and usage evidenced by available facts, as well as legal and historical development will be examined in the remaining pages of this book.

CHAPTER II

HISTORICAL BACKGROUND

In order to comprehend intelligently the present situation it is necessary to understand the events and forces which have helped form the existing pattern. It is a complex story, greatly colored by human emotion.

This chapter is divided into three parts. The first deals with the Colonial and Revolutionary period in which many basic principles were laid down. The second section spans the era following the adoption of the Federal Constitution to the close of the nineteenth century in which the basic principles were tested many times and new concepts emerged. The third section focuses on the twentieth-century forces that challenge older concepts.

COLONIAL TO CONSTITUTIONAL PERIOD

When the first settlers reached this country, they were not, upon stepping onto the soil of the New World, immediately transformed from Europeans into "Americans." They were still Englishmen, Dutchmen, Swedes, or Frenchmen separated only geographically from their original homes. They brought with them attitudes, training, and tradition from their national backgrounds. In the matter of the relationship of church and state the prevailing system in Europe was one of close cooperation between the state and a single church. In all the European states at the time of the early immigration to America a religious establishment was enforced. Germany was divided primarily between Lutheranism and Catholicism, depending on the inclination of the ruler of each area. Holland legally endorsed the Dutch Reformed Church; England, the Church of England; Sweden, the Lutheran Church; and Scotland, the Presbyterian Church. Settlers transferred these churches to their new homes in the colonies. The Anglican Church was legally established in Virginia and the Carolinas, the Dutch Reformed Church in New Netherland, the Lutheran Church in Delaware, and the Congregational and Presbyterian churches in New England. There were regions such as Rhode Island, Maryland, and Pennsylvania where more religious freedom was allowed, but for the majority of American colonies establishment was the rule.

4

Among the colonists establishment was commonly understood to mean the following two things: 1. The state gave financial support to the church through allocation of a portion of tax money or through gifts of public lands. 2. The state enforced by law the public worship and doctrines of the established church with punishment for offenders or for deviations from its worship and doctrine.

From the very earliest colonial times it was assumed that the state could dictate to its people on religious matters, although some settlers protested this prerogative. Most note-worthy of the nonconformists was Roger Williams, who was banished from Massachusetts for his differences with the authorities. He founded Rhode Island and made there a haven for persons of all beliefs. Williams contended that not only should everyone be allowed to worship God as his conscience dictated, but that those who did not believe in God should be able to practice their nonbelief.

Roger Williams' idea of religious freedom represented a minority opinion but it took root and increased in strength as more dissenting groups came to the American colonies.

In Rhode Island no tax money was used to support churches. In 1716 a law stated: "What maintenance or salary may be thought needful or necessary by any churches, congregations or societies . . . for the support of . . . their ministers may be raised by a free contribution and no other ways.[1]

The effect of establishment on education in the colonies is obvious. Where schools were founded, religious conformity was taught and enforced. In the elementary school, instruction was centered on the "three R's" and the rudiments of religious faith. The hornbook, most commonly used reading material, was a parchment on which the alphabet, some syllables, a benediction, and the Lord's Prayer was printed. Another widely read religious text, written by the famous minister John Cotton, was a catechism bearing the imposing title: *Spiritual Milk for American Babes Drawn Out of the Breasts of Both Testaments for Their Souls' Nourishment.*

By far the most extensively used text of the period was the *New England Primer*, a best-seller even by modern standards, boasting sales of three million copies from 1700 to 1850.[2] It began with the alphabet in capital and lower case letters, each letter illustrated and accompanied by a well-known rhyme of religious nature. From the word lists, which were always of a moral or religious character, the student progressed to other readings such as the Lord's Prayer, the Apostles'

Creed, the Ten Commandments, the books of the Bible, and the Shorter Westminster Catechism.

An early school law in America was passed in 1647 in Massachusetts. The religious motivation behind it is expressed in the preamble: "It being one chiefe project of that ould deluder Satan, to keepe men from the knowledge of ye Scriptures, as in former times by keeping them in an unknown tongue . . . It is therefore ordered, that every township in this jurisdiction after the Lord hath increased it to the number of fifty householders, shall forthwith appoint one within their town to teach all such children as shall resort to him to read and write . . . "³

This Massachusetts law introduced the principle of public control of education which is important in the nineteenth century struggle over religion in education. The pattern in the South differed from that of New England. Except for the education of the poor in charity schools the means of formal training were private. Following the pattern of English education, both public and private schools were supervised by the Anglican Church which reserved the right to approve teachers.

Much attention was given to the selection and control of teachers. Approval of teaching personnel was secured in somewhat different ways in various sections of the country. In New England teachers were approved by town meetings, selectmen, school committees, and ministers. In the Middle Colonies teaching certificates were issued by royal governors, royal proprietors, and religious groups. Teachers in the Southern Colonies were certified by the governors, parish officials, and religious agencies. The three most important requirements were: (1.) religious orthodoxy, (2.) loyalty to the civil government, and (3.) morals of an acceptable standard.

The earliest tradition in the development of colonial schools was obviously not one of separation at all but of close cooperation between religion and education. Those who argue at the present time for the inclusion of more religion in the public schools refer to this period as one which sets a precedent for their point of view.

With the passing of time, a gradual change took place throughout colonial America, and state sanction for a number of churches in each colony became common practice. This has been called the era of multiple establishment. During the first wave of immigration, most of the settlements were religiously homogeneous. In the years which followed, however, not only did persons of other faiths come to religiously homogeneous colonies, but population movements among the settlements brought persons of differing religious beliefs together. This naturally brought about a demand that citizens who did not believe in the system of faith and worship endorsed by the state should not be forced to support it. The "Great Awakening" which swept the colonies during the middle years of the eighteenth century stimulated the growth of Baptist, Methodist, and Presbyterian denominations which believed in a free and close association of each person with his Creator. These increasingly important dissenting groups struggled against single establishment.

The first step toward multiple establishment came when it ceased to be a crime to attend a church other than the established one. Persons living in the colony were still forced to support the state church through their taxes. Another step was taken with the acceptance of the principle that towns could, by election, determine which church would be supported by municipal revenues. This was an opening wedge allowing dissenting groups to levy taxes for support of their own denominational bodies. An example of this movement can be seen in New York when the English took over the colony following the Dutch Wars. The "Dukes Laws" of 1664 required each township to support a minister, but the denomination was to be determined by majority vote.[4]

The final step in the direction of multiple establishment was taken when a variety of religious groups were granted government approval to receive tax support for their activities. In many cases these groups were Protestant only, with Roman Catholic and Jewish believers excluded. The South Carolina constitution of 1778 stated: "The Christian Protestant religion shall be deemed and is hereby constituted and declared to be the established religion of this State. That all denominations demeaning themselves peaceably and faithfully shall enjoy equal religious and civil privileges."[5]

This period of multiple establishment has been cited by some writers as precedent for state cooperation with all religious bodies impartially. To others, however, it is simply a transitional step from state support of a single religious faith to complete freedom of religion.

The struggle for separation of church and state in America took place largely in the eighteenth century. Although initiated on the federal level upon ratification of the Bill of Rights by two-thirds of the states, it was not completely accepted as a state principle until 1833, when Massachusetts abolished compulsory support of religion.

The idea of the separation of church and state received an increasing

number of adherents during the third quarter of the eighteenth
century. Several forces contributed to its growing popularity.

First, the "Great Awakening" had stimulated colonial interest in
religion particularly of the "popular" type. Such denominations as
Presbyterians, Baptists, and Methodists which emphasized personal
religious freedom grew in numbers. These groups believed that
religion was a matter between God and the individual and was not
something to be legislated by men. Samuel Staymen, minister of
the First Baptist Church of Boston, preached from the pulpit that,
"the jurisdiction of the magistrate neither can nor ought to be extended to the salvation of souls." [6] Isaac Backus, spokesman for the
Massachusetts Baptist churches during the Revolutionary War and
constitutional period, sounded a similar note when he wrote: "The
free exercise of private judgment and inalienable rights of conscience
are too high a rank and dignity to be submitted to the decrees of
councils or the imperfect laws of fallible legislators. Religion is a
concern between God and the soul with which no human authority
can meddle." [7]

A few years before the adoption of the First Amendment to the
Constitution, the Presbyterian Church took this stand: "Religion is
altogether personal and the right of exercising inalienable: and it is
not, cannot, and ought not to be resigned to the will of society at large;
and much less to the legislature." [8]

"God alone," a leader of the Congregational Church stated, is the
God of consience and consequently attempts to erect human tribunals
for the consciences of men are impious encroachments upon the pre-
rogatives of God." [9]

The sentiment of a number of religious groups was thus not in favor
of governmental assistance but of complete separation of government
and religion.

The second force which worked for separation was the growing
multiplicity of denominations and sects. Rivalries were sharp and dis-
sensions numerous because of the jealousies created by multiple
establishment. Each sect, fearful that some other would be unduly
favored, clamored loudly for consideration.

The third and possibly the most important force for separation was
the influence of the Age of Enlightenment. Among the more influential
doctrines of eighteenth-century Enlightenment was the one concerning
the "natural rights of man." When applied to matters of religion,
"natural rights" meant more than simply a toleration of dissenting
belief. As long as the state had the right to sit in judgment of the

worth of any religious faith or to force citizens to pay taxes to support
a teaching in which they did not believe, there would be no equal
rights of conscience. A person was to be judged on his morality, not
his religion. Among those who accepted this concept were such
leaders as James Madison, Thomas Paine, and Thomas Jefferson, all of
whom fought hard for complete separation of church and state on both
state and national levels.

When the thirteen colonies declared themselves free from England
and became thirteen states, the notion of the separation of church
and state was incorporated in a number of their constitutions. This
action furnished an example and a precedent which was followed
when the First Amendment was adopted.

At the time the United States Constitution was ratified, nine of the
original thirteen states had virtual separation in their state constitutional provisions. Only four still permitted the use of public funds
to support religious worship and ministers: Maryland, which abolished
establishment in 1810; Connecticut, which abolished it in 1818; New
Hampshire, in 1819; and Massachusetts, in 1833.

While the majority of individual states had denied government
assistance to sectarian religion at the time of the Constitutional Convention in 1787, it was by no means certain what stand the Convention would take on the matter. When finally completed, the Constitution contained only one sentence regarding religion. This was
the restriction, found in Article VI, that religious tests could not be
made a qualification for public office. Demands were voiced from
many quarters that a more thoroughgoing statement on individual
rights be included in the Constitution.

When the Bill of Rights was being drafted by the first Congress,
Madison proposed that guarantees of religious freedom be imposed
on both the federal and state governments. While the restriction on
the states was not acted upon, his suggestion that the federal government could not establish a religion or infringe on the free exercise of
religion was given a favorable reception by Congress, and action was
begun to put it into law. There were a number of changes in the wording of the bill and a great amount of argument took place before the
final phraseology was accepted. Madison felt that the great rights of
the people were liberty in religious matters, trial by jury, and freedom
of the press. These freedoms became part of the wording of the First
Amendment as finally drawn:

"Congress shall make no law respecting an establishment of religion,
or prohibiting the free exercise thereof: or abridging the freedom of

speech, or of the press, or the right of the People to peaceably assemble
and petition the Government for a redress of grievances."

This provision committed the federal government to the principle
of separation of church and state even though not all the individual
states had embraced the idea at the time.

It is this in the law that has been referred to throughout 170 years
of American history whenever questions involving religion and public
education have been raised. It has been criticized as being too vague
and not pinpointing what was meant by "no law respecting an
establishment of religion." The proponents of close cooperation
between church and state maintain the amendment does not prohibit
impartial governmental assistance to all religious groups, while strict
separationists hold that even religious inscriptions on coins and the
prayers of chaplains in Congress violate the intent of the law. The
debate will probably continue for a long time. As cases regarding
religion and public education reach the Supreme Court, the decisions
of that body will help clarify the specific constitutional limitations to
be placed on school systems.

EARLY NATIONAL TO MODERN PERIOD

This next period spans the years following the adoption of the
Constitution to the first years of the twentieth century, when the public
school system evolved from the private system prevailing during
pre-Revolutionary times. Since education is one of the rights not
claimed in the Constitution by the federal government, it was
placed in the hands of the states, and for this reason there was no
uniform policy on the place of religion in the new public schools.

The public education movement grew rather slowly following the
Revolutionary War but gained momentum during the first half of the
nineteenth century. Since this country had become a democracy it
was necessary to insure an educated electorate to control the destiny of
the republic. The best method of education was through universal
schooling available to all. If education was to be universal, it would
have to be free; if it was to be free, it would have to be state supported.
A system of education supported by public taxation could not teach
religion without violating the primary principle of the First Amendment to the Federal Constitution. Also implicit in the First Amendment
is the second principle, that public funds could not be granted to
support religious schools. Throughout the intervening years some

aspect of one or the other of these two principles has been the source of controversy in the area of religion and education.

Opposition to the idea that religion could not be taught in the public schools came from both Protestant and Roman Catholic groups. The fight of Horace Mann in Massachusetts epitomizes the struggle against sectarian teaching in public education. He has been credited by many as the person chiefly responsible for secular schools in America. Mann did not fight for a new principle — although attacked, it had already been well established before he became active in educational matters.

By 1826 there were almost five times as many children in the public schools of Massachusetts as in private schools.[10] The heterogeneity of religious belief among the school population contributed to the provision in the Massachusetts Act of 1827 allowing school committees to select textbooks provided such books did not favor any religious sect or tenet. Mann set out to enforce this part of the statute and was criticized and abused for his efforts. The American Sunday School Union wished to have their books included as reading matter in the schools but Mann rejected them as sectarian. As a result of this action the Union tried to oust him from his position as Secretary of the Massachusetts State Board of Education. He was supported in his stand by the governor, the state board of education, and the legislature, and eventually won the battle.

Because of his Unitarian beliefs and his efforts to maintain secular schools, Mann was accused of being anti-religious and atheistic. Yet his struggle was not against religion in the public schools but against sectarianism in education. He made his position clear when he wrote: "I am in favor of religious instruction in our schools to the extremest verge to which it can be carried without invading those rights of conscience which are established by the laws of God and guaranteed to us by the Constitution of the State."[11]

Mann felt, however, that the Bible was not a sectarian book and so long as it was read without interpretation it could be legally used in the public schools. "Had the Board," he wrote in 1849, "required me to exclude either the Bible or religious instruction, I certainly should have given them the earliest opportunity to appoint my successor."[12] This quotation demonstrates the position of those who advocated the "common elements of Christianity" approach to the teaching of morality and character in the public schools. It was contended that since the Bible was common to all Christian believers no harm could result from reading it to school children if no comment was made and if it

was allowed to speak for itself. The idea that each person can interpret the Bible for himself is, however, distinctly Protestant. The
Roman Catholic authorities protested strongly against this practice.

The Vicar-General of the Roman Catholic Diocese of New York
wrote in 1840: "The Holy Scriptures are read in the schools every
day . . . The Catholic church tells her children that they must be
taught the religion by authority—the Sects say, read the bible [sic],
judge for yourselves . . . The Protestant principle is therefore acted
upon, slily inculcated, and the schools are Sectarian." [13]

Upon this argument was based the Roman Catholic demand for
public support for their parochial schools. Catholics maintained that
their freedom of conscience and religious practice was violated when
their children were forced to listen to Bible reading without interpretation by the clergy. They felt that Catholic children could not attend
the public schools if either this "Protestantism" was taught, or if *no*
religious instruction was given. In the notable hearings before the
New York Common Council in 1841 the petition for public funds for
parochial schools was denied.

Some Protestant groups also protested the "non-sectarian" religious
instruction. In 1846 the Reverend Matthew Hale Smith issued an
attack on this policy in a sermon entitled, "The Ark of God on a New
Cart," in which he, characterized the new program as "Godless and
corrupting." [14] Such Protestants felt that only through a return to
teaching religious doctrines espoused by a majority of Christians could
the schools regain their spiritual foundations.

The demand for public tax money for private religious schools was
made in many parts of the country, especially by Roman Catholics,
Episcopalians, and Lutherans, during the period from 1830 to 1870.
While a few of these requests were granted, the vast majority were
turned down as violations of the principle of separation of church and
state. A number of state legislatures approved laws specifically
banning such aid.

After the close of hostilities in 1865 and for several decades thereafter, a striking characteristic of American religious population was
a steady increase in the non-Protestant faiths. In addition to the Irish
and German immigrants, large numbers of Italian people, mostly
Catholic in background, came to America. The Jewish population also
grew as a result of migration from Germany and the eastern European
nations. While America was still a predominately Protestant country,
the growth of these non-Protestant groups had an influence on the relation of education and religion throughout the Union. The separation

of church and state was enforced more strictly than ever, for some as a protection against Catholic interests and doctrines, but for others as a guarantee of true impartiality of treatment in religion.

The Catholics, for their part, had been building up their parochial school system as the only answer to the secularism of public schools. Catholic parents were urged by pastoral letter and official pronouncement to educate their children in parochial schools.

From the Third Plenary Council of Bishops held at Baltimore in 1884 came the following injunction: ". . . we urge and enjoin Catholic parents to provide their beloved children . . . an education which is truly Christian and Catholic . . . they therefore (should) send them to parochial schools or other truly Catholic schools, unless in particular cases the Ordinary judges that some alternative may be permitted."[15] The Roman Catholic Church has continued to support this stand and today operates a large and growing system of parochial schools, in the belief that the Catholic child must receive a Catholic education if at all possible.

Following the Civil War the Catholic Church redoubled its effort to get a share of public funds for its schools. The more pressure brought to bear, the greater became the resistance against it. Congress set forth national policy when it passed a law in 1876 requiring all new states admitted to the Union thereafter to adopt an irrevocable ordinance which not only guaranteed religious freedom but insured a system of public schools open to all children and free from sectarian control. Eight years before, in 1868, the Fourteenth Amendment had been passed through which the rights of the First Amendment were made applicable to the individual states.

By 1900 the principle of separation of church and state had gained nearly complete acceptance among the states. Whether through constitutional provision, state statute, attorney general's ruling, or court decision, prohibitions on the use of public funds for sectarian purposes and guarantees of freedom of religion were almost universal.

THE MODERN PERIOD

At the dawn of the twentieth century a relative quiet had settled upon the field of conflict. Separation of church and state had been accepted legally on a national and state level. The Roman Catholic Church, after losing the battle to obtain direct aid for their schools, had turned to building up a separate and private parochial system. Protestants seemed satisfied with the secular schools and gave general agreement to the existing program. A surface calm prevailed, but underneath explosive forces were building up which would once more bring about bitter strife.

In the twentieth century most of the important developments concerning the role of religion in public education have taken place since World War I. One notable exception, which was to have far-reaching consequences for years to come, was the so-called "released time" program for religious instruction. The main impetus for released time came from Protestant groups which felt that the Sunday schools had failed to supply enough religious education for the children under their care. An example was furnished and a precedent set when the first program of released time began operation in Gary, Indiana, in 1913. Dr. William Wirt, the superintendent of schools, considered the school as only one of several organizations and community agencies which should be used to train the child. He therefore proposed that those parents who wished to do so could allow their children to go to churches of their choice and receive training in religious doctrine and worship. They would be released for a short period each week to the ministers of the city for the instruction and thus the name "released time" was coined.

The close of World War I marks the beginning of a renewed interest in religion in America and especially in the place of religion in public education. In Protestantism this interest found emphasis in Fundamentalism and the literal interpretation of the Bible. The Fundamentalists believed that more religion was necessary in all phases of American life and particularly in the school. They wished that so-called irreligious influences be removed from the schools. Their efforts to make the teaching of evolution illegal resulted in the famous Scopes trial of 1925.

An influential movement in Protestantism after World War I was Neo-orthodoxy. The disillusionment and pessimism brought on by a world conflict and by economic depression encouraged a return to the basic orthodox Protestant principles of the Reformation. Moral conduct, the Neo-orthodox Protestants argued, rested firmly on religious concepts, and if children were to learn sound morals, religious teaching must be included in the schools.

Roman Catholics were again becoming interested in how religion could be fitted into public schools. The Catholic Church had grown in size and power to the extent that its influence was given serious consideration by all groups interested in religion and education. In 1929 Pope Pius XI issued an encyclical letter on "The Christian Education of Youth" [16] which represented the official Catholic position. Simply stated it maintains that every person is born into three societies: the family, the state, and the Roman Catholic Church. The duty of the family is to generate and care for offspring; the duty of the state is to look after the temporal welfare of the community; and the duty of the Church is to care for the eternal salvation of men's souls. The Catholic Church, inasmuch as it deals with supernatural affairs, has priority over both the family and the state which deal with natural affairs only. Thus the Catholic Church claims that its right to educate its children supercedes that of the state.

One aspect of the history of the relation of religion to public education remains to be mentioned—Federal aid to schools. Federal aid bills have largely been confined to the twentieth century but a few were placed before Congress earlier.

The Northwest Ordinance of 1787 stated that "Religion, morality and knowledge, being necessary to good government and the happiness of mankind, schools and the means of education shall forever be encouraged." The encouragement in this case took the form of reserving one square mile in each township for the maintenance of public schools in that area. How this was to aid religion was not stated in the Ordinance.

The Morrill Act of 1862 contained nothing about religion, but two bills introduced in Congress a few years later provoked a considerable uproar. The first of these, written by Representative Hoar of Massachusetts, would have established minimum standards for state systems of education. Opposition came from professional educators and the N.E.A. The Roman Catholic Church also attacked it. The *Catholic World* saw in the plan the means "to suppress Catholic education and gradually extinguish Catholicity in the country . . . " [17] The Hoar Bill was never acted upon by either the Senate or the House.

The second proposal, sponsored by Senator Blair of New Hampshire, was introduced five times during the period from 1880 to 1890. Its aim was to give financial aid to public schools which met specified conditions. Funds were to be used solely for nonsectarian schools. The bill never received enough support to pass both houses of Congress, and Senator Blair laid its defeat to the Roman Catholic Church, [18] although several other groups also opposed the measure.

In the twentieth century, federal aid to education became an issue in the controversy of public support of sectarian education. The Smith-Hughes Act passed in 1917 to further vocational training stated that "No portion of any moneys appropriated under this Act for the

benefit of the States shall be applied, directly or indirectly . . .
for the support of any religious or privately owned or conducted
school or college." [19]

Following World War II educational groups strongly recommended some form of federal aid without federal control. The National
Education Association and the American Council on Education both
backed moves to give states financial aid to education. To this end
a number of bills have been introduced over the past several years
embodying various aid proposals. These bills fall into three categories:

1. Those which would deny federal aid to sectarian schools even
for "auxiliary services."

2. Those which would allow federal aid to sectarian schools for
auxiliary services.

3. Those which would give the funds to states and allow them to use
the money in any way the state constitution permitted.

The Catholic Church opposed the first type as discriminatory. Protestants and most professional educational groups opposed the second
type as a breach of the principle of separation. The third type seemed
to please no one, and such a bill never passed either house. The
disagreement between those who believe in separation of church and
state and those who feel that religion has a place in education constitutes one of the major controversies facing American education.

CHAPTER III

RELIGION AND THE LAW

The Constitution of the United States has little to say about religion, mentioning it only in Article VI, which forbids religious tests for office holders, and in the First Amendment, which prohibits any establishment of religion and insures freedom of worship. It does not deal with education since in the division of powers that right was reserved to the states in the Tenth Amendment.

The state legal codes are a different matter. Their provisions regarding education and its relation to religion vary greatly. The complexity arises not only from the differences in state law but from interpretation by both state and Federal courts.

FEDERAL LAW

Early Federal Laws Outside the Constitution. The first national law dealing with religion was passed in 1787 by Congress under the Articles of Confederation and indicated the general tenor of feeling at the time. It was contained in the "Ordinance of 1787" referring to the Northwest Territory, and provided that "no person demeaning himself in a peaceable and orderly manner shall ever be molested on account of his mode of worship or religious sentiments in the said territory." [1]

Skipping over the First Amendment which will be examined shortly, the provisions of the Louisiana Purchase Treaty of 1803 included the stipulation that until the inhabitants of the territory were admitted into citizenship they were "to be maintained and protected in the free enjoyment of their liberty, property and the religion which they profess." [2]

Treaties which the federal government makes with other countries have the same force as law to the inhabitants of the United States as is stated in Article VI of the Constitution. The United States from 1795 to 1930 signed fifty-nine treaties with other nations in which guarantees of religious liberty are found. [3]

An indirect guarantee of religious freedom is found in Article VI of the Constitution which in part states that "no religious test shall ever be required as qualification to any office of public trust under

17

the United States." This provision in effect implied freedom of worship but it has not been extensively cited by the courts because of the more explicit wording of the First Amendment.

The First Amendment to the Constitution. Madison, who submitted the original wording of the First Amendment, envisaged restrictions upon the states as well as on Congress. The House agreed with this idea but the Senate did not. Had Madison's original amendment passed the Senate the need for the Fourteenth Amendment would not have arisen. Changes in the phrasing of the final version included a restriction on Congress only, omission of the rights of conscience guarantee, and inclusion of the rights of freedom of speech, press, assembly, and petition. As finally adopted, the First Amendment read: "Congress shall make no Law respecting an establishment of religion, or prohibiting the free exercise thereof; or abridging the freedom of Speech, or of the Press; or the right of the People peaceably to assemble and petition the Government for a redress of Grievances."

Upon ratification by two-thirds of the states it became the law of the land in 1791. This experiment in religious liberty became one of the hallmarks of American democracy and throughout our history its guarantees have been called upon many times.

Sources of Authority Other Than Law. The courts occasionally cite as evidence in their decisions such things as letters, speeches, books, and other sources which are not derived from either law or prior cases. In rulings on the matter of religion in public education reference is often made to Madison's "Remonstrance" and to Jefferson's letter to the Danbury Baptists.

Madison's argument against any connection between church and state is expressed in his *Memorial and Remonstrance Against Religious Assessments.* He maintains that every man has an inalienable right to freedom of conscience. Free exercise of religion, he insists, must rest upon this natural right and not upon the pleasure of the state. While not a law, it does represent the thinking of a man instrumental in the adoption of laws relating to church and state and is therefore considered important legal evidence.

Jefferson's letter to the Danbury Baptist Association, written in 1802 while he was President of the United States, represents, as Butts points out,[4] his carefully considered opinion: "Believing with you that religion is a matter which lies solely between man and his God, that he owes account to none other for his faith or his worship, that the legislative powers reach actions only and not opinions, I contemplate with sovereign reverence that act of the whole American people which declared that their legislature should: make no law respecting an establishment of religion, or prohibiting the free exercise thereof: thus building a wall of separation between church and state." [5] The phrases "wall of separation" and "separation of church and state" are quoted in innumerable books, articles in journals, legal decisions, and addresses as epitomizing the idea of complete religious freedom under the First Amendment.

The Fourteenth Amendment and Religious Freedom. The First Amendment affects only Congress. To prevent the states from passing laws abridging civil liberties, the Fourteenth Amendment was passed by Congress and ratified by two-thirds of the states in 1868. The core of the Amendment is contained in the following quotation from the first section: "No State shall make or enforce any law which shall abridge the privileges or immunities of citizens of the United States; nor shall any State deprive any person of life, liberty, or property, without due process of law; nor deny to any person within its jurisdiction the equal protection of the laws."

For a time after it was passed, the Fourteenth Amendment was not applied to cases involving freedom of religion in the various states. It was so interpreted for the first time by the Supreme Court in 1923 in the case of Meyer v. Nebraska. The decision includes the following statement: "Without doubt it ['liberty', in the Fourteenth Amendment] denotes not merely freedom from bodily restraint but also the right of the individual to contract, to engage in any of the common occupations of life, to acquire useful knowledge, to marry, to establish a home, and bring up children, to worship God according to the dictates of his own conscience, and to generally enjoy those privileges long recognized at common law as essential to the orderly pursuit of happiness by free men." [6]

In subsequent cases Pierce v. Society of Sisters in 1925, Minersville School District v. Gobitis in 1940, and others—the freedom of religion expressed in the First Amendment has been applied to the states under the authority of the Fourteenth Amendment.

In 1876 a law was passed by Congress which required all new states admitted to the Union to guarantee religious freedom and also to set up a system of public education free from sectarian control. Thus again the principle of separation of church and state is reaffirmed by law on the federal level and made binding on the states seeking admission to the Union after 1876.

Federal Aid Acts. During the twentieth century a number of resolutions were submitted to Congress which involved religion and public education. The Smith-Hughes Act of 1917, by which the federal government helped the states with home economics, agriculture, and industrial arts in public schools, stipulates that the money given to the states cannot be used directly or indirectly in religious schools. The School Lunch Act of 1946, on the other hand, allows such funds to be spent in parochial schools. Another such measure, the National Defense Education Act of 1958, gives money to public and private schools alike for the improvement of certain specified programs such as guidance activities, science equipment, and foreign language materials.

In contrast to these bills which deal with specific aspects of education, a number of general aid bills have been introduced and all have met defeat, a prime reason being the religious issue. The Roman Catholics feel that they are entitled to federal aid for their schools. Opposing them are Protestants and those who dislike public aid of any kind for sectarian education. Whenever a bill is satisfactory to one side, it is not acceptable to the other. Such measures as the Barden Bill, the Kelly Bill, and the Kennedy Administration Education Bill of 1961 have suffered defeat in large part because they could not satisfy both parties. Other factors have contributed to the death of such bills to be sure, but the religious issue has been paramount.

STATE LAW

The place of religion in the public school receives different treatment in the various states. All state laws expound the principle of separation, but actual practices vary from strictest separation to considerable religious, and even sectarian, influence. In all state constitutions provision is made for religious freedom; most of them include the right to worship according to conscience and the prohibition of compulsory support of religion by any individual.[7]

Two states' constitutions contain provisions which seem to be carryovers from very early constitutional times. The New Hampshire Bill of Rights, Article V, gives religious freedom to its citizens, but Article VI gives the legislature the right to "support public protestant (sic) teachers of piety, religion and morality." It further states that, "every denomination of Christian . . . shall be equally under the protection of the law."[8]

Vermont likewise guarantees freedom of worship but Chapter I, Article 3 of its constitution closes with the admonition that "christians (sic) ought to observe the sabbath or Lord's day, and keep up some sort of religious worship."[9]

To illustrate briefly the variety of ways the states deal with the problem a number of the most controversial practices are listed below including some of the more common usage among the states.

Bible Reading Example of Dissimilar Law. The legal status of Bible reading serves as an example of how differently the states view this religious practice. The following material was taken from a study done in 1956 at the University of Chicago.[10]

Law Requires Bible Reading:

Alabama	Florida	Maine
Arkansas	Georgia	Massachusetts
Delaware	Idaho	New Jersey
District of Columbia	Kentucky	Pennsylvania[11]
		Tennessee

Law or Judicial Decision Specifically Permits Bible Reading:

Colorado	Michigan	North Dakota
Iowa	Minnesota	Ohio
Indiana	Nebraska	Oklahoma
Kansas	New York City	Mississippi
		Texas

*Law Permits Bible Reading Under General Terms of the
Law or by Reason of Silence:*

Connecticut		
Maryland	Oregon	Montana
Missouri	South Carolina	Rhode Island
New Hampshire	South Dakota	Virginia
North Carolina	Vermont	West Virginia

*Bible Reading Not Permitted Under Interpretation
of State Constitution or Statute:*

Arizona	Nevada	Utah
California	New Mexico	Washington
Illinois	New York (outside	Wisconsin
Louisiana	New York City)	Wyoming

A typical provision in state law which requires Bible reading is found in Section 145 of Chapter 4, Revised Statutes 1954, As Amended, the State of Maine. Parts of this section read as follows: "To insure greater security in the faith of our fathers, to inculcate into the lives of the rising generation the spiritual values necessary to the well being of our and future civilizations, to develop those high moral and religious principles essential to human happiness . . . there shall be, in all the public schools of the state daily, or at suitable intervals, reading from the scriptures with special emphasis upon the Ten Commandments, the Psalms of David, the Proverbs of Solomon, the Sermon on the Mount and the Lord's Prayer. It is further provided, that there shall be no denominational or sectarian comment or teaching and each student shall give respectful attention but shall be free in his own forms of worship." [12]

A provision of the type which specifically permits Bible reading in the public schools but does not require it is the one governing Iowa schools: "The Bible shall not be excluded from any public school or institution in the state, nor shall any child be required to read it contrary to the wishes of his parents or guardian." [13]

An example of a state code which does not permit Bible reading can be seen in Nevada law: "No books, tracts or papers of a sectarian or denominational character shall be used or introduced in any public school . . ." [14]

Free Textbooks. At present only four states use public funds to provide free textbooks for parochial students: Louisiana, Mississippi, New Mexico, and West Virginia. [15]

Most state codes contain sections allowing distribution of free textbooks to the "schools of the district," or some similar wording. The decision permitting distribution to private religious schools comes from court rulings which interpret the law as allowing textbooks for all children whether they go to public or private schools. These court rulings are covered in this chapter under the sections on state and federal court decisions.

Public Transportation. State law covering public transportation to private and parochial schools is also widely dissimilar in nature. In Kansas, Michigan, New Hampshire, New Jersey, New York, Oregon, California, Illinois, Indiana, Kentucky, Louisiana, Maryland, Massachusetts, Missouri, Rhode Island, and Wisconsin the law permits the use of public school busses for the transportation of children to schools other than public schools.

The Michigan Code shows the nature of these permissive statutes: "The board of any school district may enter into a contract with any other district or with private individuals to furnish transportation for non-resident pupils attending public, private, or parochial schools located within such district or in other districts: Provided, however, that in no event may the price paid for such transportation be less than the actual cost thereof to the district furnishing the same." [17]

The Iowa law is representative of statutes prohibiting use of public transportation for children attending private or parochial schools: "Contracts for school bus service with private parties shall be in writing and be for the transportation of children who attend public school." [18]

In a number of cases the law does not refer specifically to public schools in its wording and it is the duty of the courts to determine whether parochial school children are entitled to free transportation at public expense.

State Aid to Sectarian Schools. The majority of state constitutions contain prohibitions against public aid to sectarian schools. Thirty-six states have enacted laws similar to this one found in the constitution of Pennsylvania: "No appropriations shall be made for charitable, educational or benevolent purposes to any person or community nor to any denominational or sectarian institution corporation or association." [19]

The state codes which do not contain this type of provision are silent on the subject. This is true of the following:

Arkansas	Maryland	Tennessee
Connecticut	New Jersey	Vermont
Iowa	North Carolina	West Virginia
Maine	Rhode Island	Wisconsin

Released time programs. Released time for religious instruction has likewise received differing treatment from state legislatures. Eleven states have laws specifically permitting released time programs: California, Indiana, Kentucky, Maine, Massachusetts, Minnesota, New York, Oregon, Pennsylvania, South Dakota, and West Virginia. Typical wording is found in the South Dakota code: "A child may, on application of his parent or guardian, be excused from school for one hour a

week for the purpose of taking or receiving religious instruction conducted by some church or association of churches . . . and in no
event shall such instruction be given in whole or in part at public expense." [20]

Other state codes are silent on the issue and the courts must interpret the laws whenever the legal point of released time is raised.

Public School Use of Religious Buildings and Teachers. The practice of some school boards of designating a parochial school as a public
school and allocating public money to maintain it is not covered by
law. The cases involving this practice are decided by the courts
largely on the basis of "sectarian influence in public education" statutes. Some states have laws regulating the title to property to be
used as public school buildings which precludes employing church
property for public instruction. Such is the case in Missouri where
the state code holds that "The title of all schoolhouse sites and other
school property shall be vested in the district in which the same may
be located; and all property leased or rented for school purposes shall
be wholly under the control of the board of directors during such
time . . . " [21]

Much the same situation exists in regard to employing members of
religious orders as teachers in public schools. Thirteen states have
laws which prohibit religious tests as qualification for teachers in
public schools. An example of such a regulation is found in the
state code of Idaho: "No religious test or qualification shall ever be
required of any person as a condition of admission to any public
education institution of the state, either as teacher or student . . ." [22]

Thus the fact that the members of religious orders hold strongly
to certain beliefs does not disqualify them from teaching. Three
states feel that the habit worn by these teachers wields a sectarian influence and have passed laws prohibiting the wearing of such clothing
by public school teachers.

A Nebraska statute states: "Any teacher in any public school in the
state who shall wear in said school or while engaging in the performance of his duty any dress or garb indicating the fact that such a
teacher is a member or an adherent of any religious order, sect, or
denomination, shall be deemed guilty of a misdemeanor . . ." [23]

Other practices. The following examples illustrate how a few
states deal with lesser issues connected with religious education in
public schools. It must be borne in mind that the list does not apply

to all states, or even to the majority of states but is composed of legal regulations which have been set up in some states.

1. The Ten Commandments must be displayed in schools.

2. Sectarain influence in textbooks used in public schools is prohibited.

3. The teaching of the theory of evolution is prohibited.

4. The use of public school property by religious groups is prohibited.

5. Students may be excused from hygiene classes or physical examinations by reason of religious convictions.

6. Students may be excused from saluting the flag because of religious reasons.

7. Students may be excused from religious exercises which offend their religious beliefs.

The foregoing facts emphasize that while the law guarantees complete freedom of worship and separation of church and state, the legislatures usually tend to interpret freedom and separation in a variety of ways. A multitude of conflicting court decisions compound the confusion. The following pages are devoted to the interpretations by the courts of federal and state law.

SUPREME COURT DECISIONS

The cases covered in this section have come before the Supreme Court in the last thirty-five years and the resulting court decisions are directly concerned with the problem under discussion.

The United States Supreme Court rules primarily on questions involving violations of the Constitution and federal statutes. On occasion it has refused jurisdiction because of the lack of a federal question: if no federal laws are at issue, no Supreme Court ruling can be obtained. The high tribunal also declines to judge unless a specific violation is presented and does not presume to pass judgment on the constitutionality of state laws unless injury is shown. Many existing laws may therefore be unconstitutional as they stand but money, time, and effort have not been expended to test them by taking violations to the Court. It is nearly impossible to predict in advance what direction a ruling will take because of the changing personnel of the court and the fact that each case is decided on the basis of its own individual merits.

Meyer v. Nebraska. Following World War I, when patriotic fervor was high, a number of states passed laws requiring all instruction in public schools to be given in the English language. In this frame of mind the Nebraska legislature enacted a law in 1919 which made English the only acceptable language, in all schools, both public and private as well. Because German was spoken in several Lutheran parochial schools, the state law was appealed to the Supreme Court. In 1922 that body declared the Nebraska statute violated the "liberty" guaranteed by the Fourteenth Amendment—the constitutional rights of the teachers and parents of students—and was therefore unconstitutional. This decision set a precedent for the better known case of Pierce v. Society of Sisters which came before the high court three years later.

Pierce v. Society of Sisters. The Pierce case came about when Oregon passed an act in 1922 requiring all children, with a few exceptions on the basis of abnormality, to attend a public school. Exemptions from this rule could be obtained by requesting of the county superintendent of schools permission to attend a private school and by submitting to him for an examination. Two organizations which conducted private schools challenged the constitutionality of the act and took the case through to the Supreme Court. The appellees, the Society of Sisters of the Holy Names of Jesus and Mary, and the Hill Military Academy were fearful that the law would drive all private and religious schools out of business in Oregon. The suit rested somewhat on business considerations and the loss of students and property value. Partially on the basis that the state has no right to interfere in legitimate business enterprises, the law was declared unconstitutional. In the majority opinion delivered by Justice McReynolds, the Court reaffirmed the principle laid down in the Meyer case that the state cannot tell parents where to school their children. Part of the decision reads:

"Under the doctrine of Meyer v. Nebraska, 262 U.S. 390 we think entirely plain that the Act of 1922 unreasonably interferes with the liberty of parents and guardians to direct the upbringing and education of children under their control . . . The child is not the mere creature of the State; those who nurture him and direct his destiny have the right, coupled with the high duty, to recognize and prepare him for additional obligations." [24]

Another quotation shows the commercial nature of the suit: "Appellees are corporations and therefore, it is said, they cannot claim for themselves the liberty which the Fourteenth Amendment guarantees.

Accepted in the proper sense this is true . . . But they have businesses and property for which they claim protection. These are threatened with destruction through the unwarranted compulsion which appellants are exercising over present and prospective patrons of their schools." [25]

The decision was regarded as the "Magna Charta" of the private schools and encouraged the expansion of such institutions, especially Catholic parochial schools. Since the Meyer and Pierce cases the private school has continued to be an important factor in the education of American children.

Cochran v. Board of Education. With their position thus made sound, the Catholic parochial school authorities began to seek indirect aid from public funds. This was done through the logic of the "child benefit theory" which, in essence, maintains that students attending any school, parochial or public, are entitled to certain grants of tax money on the basis that it is the child who benefits, not the school. This theory was tested in Louisiana in 1929 where the legislature had passed a law which provided free textbooks for all the children of the state. Money for the purchase of such books was given to parochial schools by the state school authorities.

The Louisiana constitution, however, contained a provision against using public funds for support of private or sectarian schools. A taxpayer named Cochran charged that he was being taxed to support secetrian religion. The Louisiana State Supreme Court ruled against him and he appealed to the U.S. Supreme Court. Chief Justice Hughes prepared the majority opinion supporting the lower court.

The decision of the U.S. Supreme Court pointed out: "One may scan the acts in vain to ascertain where any money is appropriated for the purchase of school books for the use of any church, private, sectarian, or even public school. The appropriations were made for the specific purpose of purchasing school books for the use of the school children of the state, free of cost to them . . . The school children and the state alone (not the sectarian schools) are the beneficiaries." [26]

Insisting that it is not the school but the child which benefits by such aid, the Supreme Court encouraged further "child benefit" demands in matters of school lunches, transportation and textbooks.

Clithero v. Showalter. At about the same time the Cochran decision was handed down another case related to religion and public education was in the making. In 1930 G. I. Clithero and others filed a petition demanding that the state board of education require the teaching and reading of the Bible in the state of Washington. The State Supreme Court denied the requested writ of mandamus on the ground that it violated state constitutional provisions guaranteeing religious freedom. Clithero appealed to the U.S. Supreme Court, contending that his freedom of worship would be denied if Bible reading and teaching were not instituted. The appellees rested their case on the finding of the Washington Supreme Court that the courts cannot by mandamus control an administrative board which has discretionary powers. They also contended that Bible reading and instruction would violate the state constitution. The U.S. Supreme Court dismissed the case for lack of a substantial federal question, in effect Clithero's petition was denied.

Flag Salute Cases. The patriotism which characterized many communities shortly before the beginning of World War II was a contributing factor in another law suit involving religion and education. Litigation in the case of Minersville School District v. Gobitis began in 1938 when a federal judge ordered two pupils of the Minersville, Pennsylvania school reinstated after they had been expelled by the school authorities. The children had been instructed by their parents, members of the Jehovah's Witnesses sect, not to salute the American flag. Gobitis brought action to have his children accepted back into the public schools of Minersville. The case was pursued through the lower courts to the U.S. Supreme Court. Significantly, every court except the highest agreed with the plaintiff that forcing pupils to salute the flag was a violation of their freedom of worship. In 1940 the Supreme Court ruled that the school district did have the right to expel students for failure to salute the flag. Justice Frankfurter, who wrote the majority opinion for the court, stated the heart of the decision in this sentence: "The mere possession of religious convictions which contradict the relevant concerns of a political society does not relieve the citizen from the discharge of political responsibilities [saluting the flag]".[27]

The decision stood only three years; the Supreme Court reversed itself in 1943 when the same issue was presented in West Virginia State Board of Education v. Barnette, a case again involving the Jehovah's Witnesses. The state law of West Virginia instructed public school authorities that failure to salute the American flag was insubordination and therefore punishable. Taking the same stand as they had three years before in Pennsylvania, the witnesses challenged the law. The

District Court held against them, but the U.S. Circuit Court overruled the lower court. In the highest court of the land the appellants were upheld by a decision ruling that children were not required to salute the flag if it conflicted with their religious beliefs. In the majority opinion, written by Justice Jackson, the Supreme Court stated: "We think the action of the local authorities in compelling the flag salute and pledge transcends constitutional limitations on their power and invades the sphere of intellect and spirit which it is the purpose of the First Amendment to our Constitution to reserve from all official control." [28]

X   *Everson v. Board of Education.* The "child benefit theory" was given another Supreme Court test through the case of Everson v. Board of Education in 1947.[29] A statute passed in New Jersey in 1941 allowed local school boards to provide transportation for children attending both public and private schools which were not operated for profit. In one township of the state the school board reimbursed Catholic parents for the expense they incurred in transporting their children to parochial schools. Everson, a taxpayer of that district, brought suit to challenge these payments on the ground that they violated both state and federal constitutions. After lower court decisions both in favor of and against Everson, the case finally reached the Supreme Court. In a five-to-four decision the high tribunal found that no violation of the national constitution had occurred in that the financial aid did not benefit the schools but the children.

Justice Black, writing for the majority of the Supreme Court, held that "state-paid policemen, detailed to protect children going to and from church schools from the very real hazards of traffic would serve much the same purpose and accomplish much the same result as state provisions intended to guarantee free transportation of a kind, which the state deems to be best for the school children's welfare . . ." He added:

"This Court has said that parents may, in the discharge of their duty under state compulsory education laws, send their children to a religious rather than a public school if the school meets the secular educational requirements which the state has the power to impose. See Pierce v. Society of Sisters, 268 U.S. 510. It appears that these parochial schools meet New Jersey's requirements. The State contributes no money to the schools. It does not support them. Its legislation, as applied does no more than provide a general program to help parents get their children, regardless of their religion, safely and expeditiously to and from accredited schools.

"The First Amendment has erected a wall between church and state. That wall must be kept high and impregnable. We could not approve the slightest breach. New Jersey has not breached it here." [30]

Delivering the minority opinion, Justice Rutledge wrote: "Here parents pay money to send their children to parochial schools and funds raised by taxation are used to reimburse them. This not only helps the children to get to school and the parents to send them. It aids them in a substantial way to get the very thing which they are sent to the particular school to secure, namely, religious training and teaching. Without buildings, without equipment, without library, textbooks and other materials, and without transportation to bring teacher and pupil together in such an effective teaching environment, there can be not even the skeleton of what our times require . . . Payment of transportation is no more, nor is it any the less essential to education, whether religious or secular than payment for tuitions, for teachers' salaries, for buildings, equipment and necessary materials." [31]

McCollum v. Board of Education. Only one year passed before the Supreme Court was again called upon to rule on an alleged violation of the First and Fourteenth Amendments. In the case of McCollum v. Board of Education, Mrs. McCollum, an atheist, challenged the practice of the Champaign, Illinois, board of education is allowing sectarian religious teachers to come into the public school buildings and provide denominational education during school hours. She charged that this joint public school-religious group violated the constitutional provisions of religious freedom. Upon appeal through the courts to the United States Supreme Court, the decision of the Illinois supreme court was reversed and the writ of mandamus requested by Mrs. McCollum was ordered.

Justice Black, speaking for the majority of the Supreme Court, said: "The foregoing facts, without reference to others that appear in the record, show the use of tax-supported property for religious instruction and the close cooperation between the school authorities and the religious council in promoting religious education . . . This is beyond all question a utilization of the tax-established and tax supported public school system to aid religious groups to spread their faith. And it falls squarely under the ban of the First Amendment (made applicable to the States by the Fourteenth, as we interpreted it in Everson v. Board of Education, 330 U.S. 1 . . .)" [32]

The fact that the state's tax-supported public school buildings were used for the dissemination of religious doctrines was emphasized in the decision of the Court. This practice has a bearing on the next case to be discussed, where school buildings were not used for religious teaching.

Zorach v. Clauson. This case, appealed to the Supreme Court in 1952, four years after the McCollum ruling, had elements in common with the Champaign case. The released time education plan employed in New York City public schools used school hours for religious classes and the public schools kept attendance records on them. As in the Champaign schools, the students were released only on the authorization of their parents. However, here no public school property was involved. All pupils went to religious centers away from the public school building to receive denominational teaching.

The two petitioners were not atheists. Tessim Zorach belonged to the Episcopal Church and Esta Gluck was affiliated with the Jewish faith. They asserted in their complaint that because of the compulsory education law of New York and the practice of keeping records of attendance at sectarian religious classes the schools of New York were assisting religious groups to spread their faith. Contending that coercion was used to obtain attendance at these classes, they pointed out that those children who did not take part in released time education were kept in school during the period the instruction was carried on.

The Supreme Court ruled that a real difference existed between the released time programs of Champaign and New York City. It held that no assistance was given sectarian groups by the New York schools and that no coercion was employed to obtain attendance. Justice Douglas represented the majority opinion: "When the state encourages religious instruction or cooperates with religious authorities by adjusting the schedule of public events to sectarian needs it follows the best of our traditions . . . But we find no constitutional requirement which make it necessary for government to be hostile to religion and to throw its weight against efforts to widen the effective scope of religious influence." [33]

Each of three dissenting justices submitted separate opinions in which they held that coercion did exist and that the New York program should have been declared unconstitutional..

Doremus Case. This case was decided in the same year as the

Zorach case. The principle involved here was the reverse of that in Clithero v. Showalter namely, that Bible reading should be prohibited in the public schools. New Jersey law requires reading from the Old Testament portion of the Bible without comment at the beginning of each school day. The appellees, Mr. Doremus and Mrs. Klein, asked for a declaratory judgment on the constitutionality of the law. When the case was taken before the Supreme Court that body would not accept jurisdiction since Mrs. Klein's daughter had graduated from high school before the appeal was made. Other reasons were advanced by the Court for refusal to rule on the case. Mrs. Klein had made no assertion of injury or of violation of constitutional rights. She could not claim that she was forced to financially support religion since she did not allege Bible reading added to the cost of public education. Doremus could not show that he was forced to support religion against his will. On the ground that no injury was established the Supreme Court refused a decision on the case.

In a far-reaching decision on June 25, 1962, the Court held that a short non-denominational prayer used in New York schools was unconstitutional. The case centered on a 22 word prayer recommended by the New York board of regents as a devotional exercise to begin the school day. The students were not required to participate and could leave the room if they so wished. The plaintiffs contended that this ritual violated the First Amendment and the Supreme Court agreed with them.

Justice Black, writing for the majority, maintained the prayer was in effect an establishment of religion and could not be tolerated. The main consideration in this case, he held was the fact that a governmental body had written and sponsored an official prayer. While stating its opposition to this activity the Court also made it clear that it was not banning all religious references from the schools.

Justice Potter Stewart wrote the lone dissenting opinion in which he pointed out numerous instances of governmental policy and procedure where prayers, oaths and mottoes include religious references.

The size of the majority vote coupled with the non-sectarian nature of the prayer brings up the possibility that other practices used in public schools may be found illegal. New rulings will be awaited with great interest as further defining the legality of religious observances in the public schools.

At the present time the Supreme Court decisions seem to say the following:

1. The compulsory education requirements of the states need not be

fulfilled solely in public schools; these requirements can also be satisfied in private and religious schools.

2. Grants of tax money which aid children in obtaining an education and in protecting them from hazards in pursuit of education do not violate the federal Constitution, regardless of whether the school the students attend is public or religious.

3. The state does not have the right to force a display of devotion to a patriotic symbol such as the flag if such practice violates religious beliefs.

4. The "released time" program of religious education adopted in many communities is illegal if it is operated on school property or if public funds are used to further it. If the school buildings are not used and no tax money is involved, released time is permissible.

5. Official prayers written and sponsored by any arm of government cannot be used in the public schools as a devotional exercise.

In the coming years it is probable that the Supreme Court will be asked to rule on other religious practices in the schools. Increasing interest of church groups and some educational associations will bring about new attempts to put more emphasis on religion in the public schools. Resistance to practices already in common use in many states may result in a testing of their legality before the high court. The nature of Court rulings cannot be determined in advance, but it is reasonable to assume that the First and Fourteenth Amendments will be subjected to further interpretation in the not-too-distant future.

STATE COURT DECISIONS

With fifty states having varying constitutional and legal provisions regarding the place of religion in the schools, the field is indeed a complicated one. The state laws respecting public education alone are extensive. Add to this the wide range of religious implications which could apply to these statutes and any complete analysis becomes impossible. The plan of this discussion will be to identify a number of the main and recurring problems which the state courts have been called upon to decide. Under each problem will be examples of decisions showing how the various tribunals have viewed the questions. The coverage cannot be complete because of limitations of space, but it can demonstrate the complexity and diverse nature of the relationship.

Bible Reading in Public Schools.   The question of whether the
reading of the Bible in public schools violates the constitutional rights
of citizens has been tested many times in the state courts.   As was
pointed out in the last section, the United States Supreme Court has
refused to rule on the two cases presented to it.   Many of the state
cases have been brought by Roman Catholics or Jews who objected to
the King James version of the Bible.   The Roman Catholics believe
that the Douay translation is the only valid and sacred Bible, while
the Jews consider both versions inaccurate and misleading and do
not feel the New Testament to be the word of God.   Freethinkers and
atheists maintain that while the Bible may be a great literary book,
it is sectarian since it is the base of the Judaic and Christian religions.

The defenders of Bible reading in the public schools argue that
the moral and ethical traditions of western civilization come from the
Bible and therefore it should be read to school children.   When this is
done without comment or interpretation, no sectarian teaching takes
place and no beliefs are violated.

In an earlier part of this chapter the wide variations in state law
regarding Bible reading are pointed out.   The court decisions also
show widely differing opinions on the legality of the practice.   The
majority of rulings have found that Bible reading is not a sectarian
practice and have allowed its continued use in public schools.   Such
has been the opinion of the courts in Georgia, Colorado, Florida, Iowa,
Kentucky, Maine, Massachusetts, Minnesota, Nebraska, New York,
Ohio, Pennsylvania, Tennessee, and Texas.[34]   An example of such a
decision is found in the case of Wilkerson v. City of Rome heard before
the Supreme Court of Georgia in 1921.   In its opinion the court said:
"It would require a strained and unreasonable construction to find anything in the ordinance which interferes with the natural and inalienable right to worship God according to the dictates of ones own
conscience.   The mere listening to the reading of an extract from the
Bible and a brief prayer at the opening of school exercises would
seem far remote from such interference." [35]

In 1956 a Tennessee court ruled on the place of the Bible in the
public schools of that state.   It had been the custom of some schools
to keep records of attendance at Sunday School and require absentees
to copy portions of the Bible on Monday.   The court declared this
action was not within the authority of school boards, but that singing
of hymns, reading the Bible without comment, and repeating the
Lord's Prayer did not violate the state or federal constitutions.[36]

Contrary opinion has been expressed by courts in the states of Wis-

consin, Illinois, Louisiana, South Dakota, Pennsylvania, and Washington.[37] The Illinois decision stated: "It is true this is a Christian
state. The great majority of its people adhere to the Christian religion.
No doubt this is a Protestant state . . . But the law knows no distinc-
tion between the Christian and the Pagan, the Protestant and the
Catholic. All are citizens. Their civil rights are precisely equal. The
school, like the government, is simply a civil institution. It is secular
not religious in its purposes. The truths of the Bible are the truths
of religion, which do not come within the province of the public
school." [38]

An interesting case which recently came up in Pennsylvania has
resulted in a decision that Bible reading is improper. The suit,
Schlempp v. School Dist. of Abington Township, Pa., 177 F. Supp.
398 (E. D. Pa. 1959); Vacated and remanded, 364 U.S. 298 (1960),
was brought to test the amended state law on Bible reading which
permits children whose parents so desire to be excused while the
Scriptures are read. A three-man federal court decided that, even
with children being excused, the reading violated the First and Fourteenth Amendments. The case was carried to the Supreme Court,
which sent it back to the lower court because the law had been amended during the suit. This legal body has again ruled the statute unconstitutional.

In nineteen states the courts have ruled on the legality of Bible reading in the light of state law. In the remaining states, decisions have
not been rendered. In view of the controversial nature of the practice,
opinions will very likely be sought in other states. It is probable that
one or more cases will be carried on to the Supreme Court, which will
render its decision on the constitutionality of the custom in public
schools.

Released Time Instruction. The legality of releasing students from
tax-supported schools to attend classes of sectarian religious instruction has been decided by several state courts. In 1925 a New York
court outlawed the Mount Vernon plan on the basis that consent
cards signed by parents were printed at public expense. It also said
that such a setup was beyond the legal powers of the board of education. The New York court of appeals, two years later, held that the
White Plains released time program was legal since no public expenditure was involved and that the school board could legally cooperate
in the plan. The supreme court of Illinois agreed with the New York
court and decided released time did not constitute sectarian teaching.

A district court of appeals in California also concurred in declaring released time to be legal. The McCollum and Zorach cases, both concerned with released time have been discussed in the preceeding section.

Legal decisions show the courts to favor released time programs when public funds or school property is not used and when pupils are not coerced to attend.

Public Schools and Church Buildings. In the matter of the use of church property for public education, as in most religious questions which courts have had to judge, there is no unanimity of opinion. In some cases the use of such property was ruled to have sectarian influence and not in others. The courts of several states: Kentucky, Iowa, Nebraska, New Mexico, and Missouri, have declared the use of church property for public schooling to be illegal. In these cases employment of religious personnel was involved and sectarian instruction had been given on public school property and during school time, considerations very probably influential in determining unconstitutionality.

Other state courts have ruled that where no sectarian teaching is done in the public school section of the building, the arrangement is legal. School boards are allowed to lease or rent church property in Iowa, Indiana, Kentucky, Illinois, Wisconsin, and Connecticut. The courts of Iowa and Kentucky have decided cases both ways: to allow rental and to disallow it. The apparent contradiction is not real when viewed from the point of view of the court. The circumstances of each case were different and the judges were in effect asked to decide whether sectarian influence was being exerted through the use of church property as a public school. Because of certain practices which were carried on in some schools and not in others, differing decisions were made.

Religious Clothing and Public School Teachers. Closely connected with this problem is the issue of employing as public school teachers, individuals who wear distinctly religious garb. The contention of those who objected to this practice was that the wearing of such clothing and symbols constituted sectarian influence in public education. Legally a teacher cannot be barred from employment on the grounds of adherence to one faith or another. To do this would violate constitutional rights. Any test therefore must be based on the possible sectarian influence of the dress.

The court decisions on the matter have, as usual, been far from uniform. A Pennsylvania court in 1894 ruled that religious garb and insignia did not have sectarian influence and those who wore them could not be excluded as teachers. As a result of this decision the state legislature passed a law prohibiting the practice and in 1910 it was declared constitutional. In New York the court of appeals decided in 1906 that religious clothing could be excluded from public schools on the basis of sectarian influence. A situation arose in North Dakota which in some respects parallels the one in Pennsylvania. The supreme court of North Dakota in 1936 ruled that the wearing of religious dress did not violate the constitution of that state. In 1948 the people of North Dakota in a referendum voted a prohibition on religious dress for public school teachers. A district court in New Mexico declared "barred forever" the Catholic nuns, brothers, and priests who up to the time of the decree in 1949, had been public school teachers in New Mexico. In addition to Pennsylvania, New York, North Dakota, and New Mexico, three other states, Arizona, Nebraska, and Oregon, have laws which prohibit religious garb in public schools.

New cases on this subject may be taken to court in the future if the shortage of teachers becomes more acute and school boards in small towns feel compelled to employ nuns and brothers as teachers.

Free Transportation to Parochial Schools. The transportation of students to parochial schools at public expense has been approved by courts in California, Maryland, Kentucky, and New Jersey. It has been declared illegal by courts in Wisconsin,[39] South Dakota, Delaware, New York, Oklahoma, Washington, and Iowa. The Kentucky supreme court through an earlier stand in 1945 found the practice legally acceptable. A New York amendment to its 1938 constitution permits parochial transportation at public expense. Most of the decisions of the state courts find that public transportation of parochial school pupils aids the school in its sectarian purpose. The supreme court of Oklahoma stated that: "The appropriation and directed use of public funds in transportation of public school children is openly in direct aid to public schools 'as such.'"[40] The Everson ruling has not had much effect on the subsequent decisions of the state supreme courts. In Iowa the supreme court through a 1947 judgment held the practice to be illegal and in 1949 the supreme court of Washington took a similar position. This shows clearly that a United States Supreme Court decision is not necessarily binding on all states but applies directly to the one in which the injury has been alleged. It is probable

that more tests of the legality of individual state laws on the transportation issue may find their way through the courts to the high tribunal.

Free Textbooks for Parochial Schools.   The "child benefit" theory,
which is the basis of favorable rulings in the above transportation cases,
is also the fundamental issue in this last question, which concerns
the practice in some states of furnishing textbooks at public expense to
children attending parochial schools.   An early New York decision in
1922 said such practice violated the meaning of the phrase "schools
of the school district" found in the *Educational Law* of New York.[41]
In the words of the ruling the following statement makes clear the point
of view of the court: "It seems to us to be giving a strained and unusual
meaning to words if we hold that the books and the ordinary school
supplies, when furnished for the use of pupils, is a furnishing to the
pupils, and not a furnishing in aid or maintenance of a school of
learning . . . It seems very plain that such furnishing is at least indirectly in aid of the institution, and that, if not in actual violation of
the words, it is in violation of the true intent and meaning of the
Constitution and in consequence equally unconstitutional." [42]

Seven years later, in 1929, the Louisiana supreme court took an
opposing view and held that when the law of Louisiana spoke of the
"school children" of the state, the term was not limited to public
school pupils only.   The court maintained that the law was general
and had been enacted for the benefit of the children themselves
and not for the schools they happened to attend.[43]   The Cochran case
decided on the same day and on the same grounds by the Louisiana
supreme court was appealed to the United States Supreme Court
which concurred in its decision.   The Mississippi supreme court held
"child benefit" to be legal in upholding a statute similar to Louisiana's.[44]

In reviewing the decisions of state courts on problems of religion
and public education, it is difficult to distinguish a pattern in the
rulings.   In some instances the courts were ruling on the interpretation of specific laws and on other occasions they were determining
if certain procedures violated general constitutional provisions.   A
person seeking legal justification for any of the six practices discussed
in this last section is able to find court decisions that support either
side of the question.

Continued litigation in the future seems almost inevitable.   Any
emerging pattern in the decisions will be anxiously watched for by
all interested parties.   Especially important will be those judgments
affecting the "child benefit" theory.

CHAPTER IV

RELIGION IN THE CURRICULUM

The school curriculum—the subject matter and organized pattern of courses which combine to make up the formal academic offerings—plays a vital role in any school. The present chapter attempts to study, from the standpoint of approach and extent of occurrence, a number of curricular practices involving religion. A general description of each practice is followed by examples illustrating typical usage. Accompanying charts show figures for communities in various population categories, for sectional areas of the country, and for the nation as a whole.

Incidental References to Religion in Coursework. Religion as a moral and philosophical concept as well as a social institution has had great influence in the history and culture not only of Western civilization but of all societies. One method of dealing with religion in the public schools is to examine objectively the dynamic force of religion. Such an approach has run into difficulty in some communities since what was viewed by the teacher as "objective teaching about religious facts" appears to be sectarian indoctrination to some clergymen and laymen. Occasionally school systems decide to omit any reference to controversial religious events to avoid arousing antagonism. F. Ernest Johnson quotes a New England school superintendent who maintained his school system had "solved" the religious problem in the teaching of history. When asked how it was done, he replied, "By omitting the Reformation." [1]

Nevertheless, many teachers do include references to religion and its influence. To handle the subject properly the instructor must be religiously literate himself. This poses a serious problem because many teachers have received little training in this area and have not spent the necessary time equipping themselves to do justice to the subject.

Several courses lend themselves well to such incidental treatment of religion as occasions arise. A great many works of art owe their inspiration to religion and the paintings themselves have religious subjects. The development of architecture cannot be studied without mention of religious influences on design and structure. In music many immortal compositions are centered on religious subjects.   School choir often sing religious pieces which consciously or unconsciously affect the singers.   Literature is filled with references to religion which cannot be avoided if the subject is to be properly taught.   It is impossible to study history without noting how religion has affected human events.   In science classes questions often arise on the relation of religion to the creation of the world, evolution, and other subjects. Course content in many subjects involves religious implications which cannot be omitted if a consideration of the area is to be complete.

When he wrote his opinion in the McCollum case Justice Jackson said: . . . "Perhaps subjects such as mathematics, physics or chemistry are, or can be, completely secularized.   But it would not seem practical to teach either practice or appreciation of the arts if we are to forbid exposure of youth to any religious influences.   Music without sacred music, architecture minus the cathedral, or painting without the scriptural themes would be eccentric and incomplete, even from a secular point of view . . . And I should suppose it is a proper, if not an indispensable, part of preparation for a worldly life to know the roles that religion and religions have played in the tragic story of mankind.   The fact is that, for good or for ill, nearly everything in our culture worth transmitting, everything which gives meaning to life, is saturated with religious influences . . . "[2]

Many school systems recognize this, and official statements as well as the attitude of school authorities encourage such reference to religion.   A typical attitude is that of an assistant superintendent of a large western city: "In the study of cultures of peoples in various countries, religion would of course be included, but it has never been singled out to receive special consideration or emphasis; neither would it be ignored or eliminated.   We would teach it as any other aspect of the cultural pattern would be handled."[3]

In a statement by the board of education of the city of New York support is also given to this widely used approach: "It should be clear that any statement on the teaching of moral and spiritual values would be inadequate and incomplete unless it gave due emphasis to the role of religious ideals in influencing moral concepts and behavior. . . Therefore the schools cannot avoid reference to the contributions of religion to the fundamental ideals which are at the very heart of our culture.[4]

Teaching Moral and Spiritual Values.   Although, strictly speaking, moral values are not classified as religious they are discussed here because some school officials, when questioned about their program of dealing with religion, mention the moral and spiritual approach. In examining a number of school publications on "moral and spiritual values" the writer has come to the conclusion that many of them should be entitled "moral values" since very little if anything on spiritual values is included. The Saint Louis public schools in their program of teaching "moral and spiritual values," emphasize such qualities as clean speech, cooperation, good will, honesty, loyalty, respect for elders, truthfulness, responsibility. A short section on reverence comprises the spiritual values.[5] Pittsburgh and Cincinnati have similar programs with the overbalancing emphasis on the moral rather than the spiritual. Such character qualities are usually taught without mention of religious sanction. An example of the position taken by some school systems can be seen in this statement by the director of elementary education of the Fairfax (Virginia) county school system: "We deal with the area of moral and spiritual values as relates to the training of good citizenship and character building of the pupils."[6] The moral and spiritual value approach can be filled with religious references but many times it stresses desirable character qualities with little emphasis on religion.

In 1955 the regents of the University of the State of New York issued a booklet containing certain recommendations for school programs.[7] Before stating any beliefs or recommendations, the regents caution school personnel to be mindful of the "fundamental American doctrine of the separation of church and state, and careful at all times to avoid any and all sectarianism or religious instruction which advocates, teaches or prefers any religious creed."[8]

The "fundamental beliefs" set forth by the regents include: (1.) Liberty under God. (2.) Respect for the dignity and rights of each individual. (3.) Devotion to freedom. In the longest section entitled "The Brotherhood of Man under the Fatherhood of God" there are many references to God in our national life. Among suggestions for implementing programs of religious emphasis are:

1. Frequent periods of study devoted to the great American documents and pronouncements. This, it is hoped, will "give to the student an understanding and appreciation of his role as an individual endowed by his Creator with inalienable rights and as a member of a group similarly endowed: of respect for others, particularly parents and teachers, of devotion to freedom and reverence for Almighty God. Thus . . . the school will fulfill its high function of supplementing the training of the home, ever intensifying in the child that love for

God, for parents and for home which is the mark of true character training and the sure guarantee of a country's welfare." [9]

2. The development of moral and spiritual values through all the activities of the day and especially by the good examples furnished by teachers. Sports and games can build a sense of fair play; science can develop a respect for truth and humility; biography supplies examples of character; and friendship among all children guard against prejudice and intolerance.

This pamphlet offers little more than a statement of policy without extensive methods for putting it into effect. It does, however, encourage a certain amount of religious emphasis in school curricula. The status of religion in public schools would be greatly clarified if state boards of education would take some stand on the subject. This would be a beginning from which school officials could proceed, making necessary adjustments for local conditions.

A program for the development of moral and spiritual ideals adopted by the board of education of the city of New York in 1956 illustrates the difficulty of obtaining agreement on such a plan. In June, 1955, the board of superintendents of the New York City public schools, following the lead of the regents, issued a report on moral and spiritual values. It included a number of references to God and presupposed the existence of a Supreme Being. Immediately after its publication, opposition developed, led by elements of the Jewish faith who labeled the program "illegal and unconstitutional." [10] As a result the board of superintendents revised the document, omitting many references to God and reducing the responsibility of the school for developing spiritual values in children. More than a year after the first statement a second one was published, this time under the authority of the board of education. Despite the changes there was still criticism, coming largely from "the major teachers' groups, the United Parents Association and the New York Board of Rabbis." [11] This second statement has not been withdrawn and stands as recommended policy in New York City schools.

Although cautioning that religious education and training may exceed the functions of public schools, the Board of Education emphasized "That any statement on the teaching of moral and spiritual values would be inadequate and incomplete unless it gave due emphasis to the role of religious ideals in influencing moral concepts and behavior." [12]

The use of general religious sanctions in the instruction is advocated: "Although religious pluralism characterizes American life, the great majority of Americans believe that God is the Author of the moral code to Whom each individual is ultimately responsible." [13]

The board of education also stressed that school rituals such as the pledge of allegiance, singing of the fourth stanza of America, reading of the Bible, use of invocations and benedictions have little meaning unless pupils are "deeply conscious of the religious underpinning of our moral and spiritual ideals." [14] The largest portion of the book contains suggestions for strengthening moral and spiritual values in the various subject matter areas, although the emphasis does not seem to be on religious sanctions.

Another experimental program provided more intensive assistance to teachers in dealing with religion in the classroom. For the past several years the Los Angeles city schools have used a guide for school personnel entitled *Moral and Spiritual Values in Education.* [15] The approach was "in terms of character values inherent in our American heritage with its background of religious faith, humanitarianism and social justice." [16] The values cited are: appreciation, cooperation, courage, faith, generosity, good will, honesty, kindness, loyalty, respect for Law, responsibility, and reverence. The roles of the principal, the teacher, and the counselor in the development of these traits are outlined in some detail. Part III of the bulletin enumerates opportunities for moral training in each of the elementary grades and in all the subject fields on the secondary level. The distinctive feature of this program is the place accorded religion, as can be seen in the preface of the bulletin: "Experiences in learning about religion are provided at appropriate times. The aim is to help students to understand the importance of religion in the lives of individuals and of nations; to understand the meaning of freedom of religion; to understand better the religious points of view of another faith; to become more loyal to the church of one's choice." [17]

To exemplify the religious emphasis of the bulletin the board of education states: "It is important also that pupils be familiar with such basic Bible passages as the Golden Rule, the Ten Commandments, the Twenty-Third Psalm, the Beatitudes. Great inspirational teachings from other religions illustrate man's search for God through the ages." [18]

The approach used throughout the entire publication is illustrated by the following passage: "No, we are not teaching religion in any sectarian sense of the word. We are regarding religion as taught in the public schools as one of the great humanities, an important factor in the life of mankind all through the ages. We are not attempting to

define religion as creed or sect, but to vitalize for young people the
great spiritual truths underlying man's search for God through the
ages." [19]

Bible quotations and references to God and religion are frequent.
In treating appreciation it is suggested that: "We need an appreciation
of God and of the importance of religion in the lives of individuals." [20]
In dealing with courage: "Boys and girls should learn that faith and
trust in God have been a source of great courage through all the ages." [21]
In the section on respect for law, the "law of love" is illustrated by
quotations from both Old and New Testaments.

The Los Angeles public schools seem to be using two approaches:
first the moral and spiritual values are being taught with the use of
religious sanctions; and second, "teaching about" religion and its
influence in human affairs is recommended to classroom teachers.
Evidently these techniques are acceptable to the people of Los Angeles,
for no widespread organized opposition has developed such as took
place in New York.

How do the school systems of the United States handle the matter
of spiritual and moral values? The results of the nation-wide poll on
this question follow.

Widespread opposition to moral values in public education is
difficult to imagine. This seems as unlikely as antipathy for home,
mother, and the flag. The results of the questionnaire bore this out.
An examination of Chart I shows how universally moral values are
emphasized in our school systems. The national average is 99.44%,
unaffected by size of community or section of the country.

However, an interesting change occurs when the question involves
spiritual values. A substantial majority of school systems do attempt
to teach spiritual values but the national percentage drops to about
75%. An exception worth noting involves the South, where 94.32% of
the replying schools include spiritual values. It seems, then, that
about one-fourth of the school systems feel spiritual values cannot
properly be included in the aims and objectives of public school
institutions.

The next survey question deals with material furnished to the
classroom teacher to assist in the teaching of moral and spiritual values.
Most of the American public school systems do provide help for
teaching moral values, although the figure here (77.51%) is not so
high as the one regarding the *aim* of such teaching. Much less help
is furnished classroom teachers for instruction in spiritual values as the
drop in the national figure to 46.34% indicates. As might be expected,

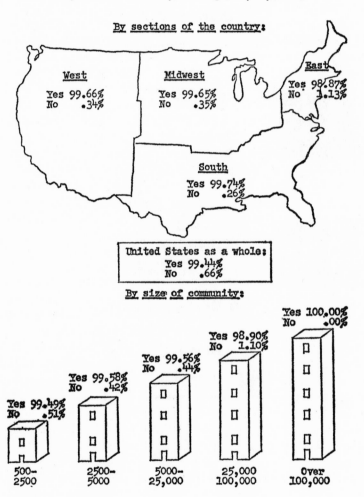

CHART I

Do the aims and objectives of your school system include the teaching of moral values? (Moral values would refer to such qualities as honesty, courage, loyalty, etc.)

By sections of the country:

West
Yes 99.66%
No   .34%

Midwest
Yes 99.65%
No   .35%

East
Yes 98.87%
No   1.13%

South
Yes 99.74%
No   .26%

United States as a whole:
Yes 99.44%
No   .66%

By size of community:

Yes 99.49%
No   .51%

Yes 99.58%
No   .42%

Yes 99.56%
No   .44%

Yes 98.90%
No   1.10%

Yes 100.00%
No   .00%

| 500-2500 | 2500-5000 | 5000-25,000 | 25,000 100,000 | Over 100,000 |

45

CHART II

Does your school system provide materials to classroom teachers to help in teaching moral values?

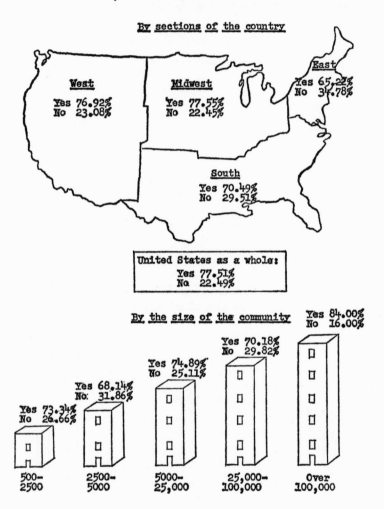

By sections of the country

West
Yes 76.92%
No 23.08%

Midwest
Yes 77.55%
No 22.45%

East
Yes 65.22%
No 34.78%

South
Yes 70.49%
No 29.51%

United States as a whole:
Yes 77.51%
No 22.49%

By the size of the community

Yes 73.34%
No 26.66%

Yes 68.14%
No: 31.86%

Yes 74.89%
No 25.11%

Yes 70.18%
No 29.82%

Yes 84.00%
No 16.00%

500–2500   2500–5000   5000–25,000   25,000–100,000   Over 100,000

CHART III

Do the aims and objectives of your school system include the teaching of spiritual values? (Spiritual values refer to such qualities as love, faith, reverence for a Supreme Being, etc.)

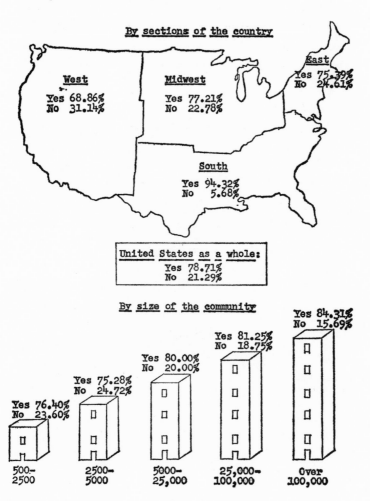

By sections of the country

West
Yes 68.86%
No 31.14%

Midwest
Yes 77.21%
No 22.78%

East
Yes 75.39%
No 24.61%

South
Yes 94.32%
No 5.68%

United States as a whole:
Yes 78.71%
No 21.29%

By size of the community

Yes 76.40%
No 23.60%

Yes 75.28%
No 24.72%

Yes 80.00%
No 20.00%

Yes 81.25%
No 18.75%

Yes 84.31%
No 15.69%

500-2500

2500-5000

5000-25,000

25,000-100,000

Over 100,000

47

CHART IV

Does your school system provide materials to classroom teachers to help in teaching spiritual values?

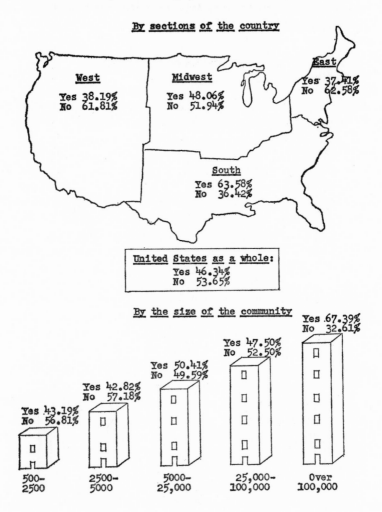

By sections of the country

East
Yes 37.41%
No 62.58%

West
Yes 38.19%
No 61.81%

Midwest
Yes 48.06%
No 51.94%

South
Yes 63.58%
No 36.42%

United States as a whole:
Yes 46.34%
No 53.65%

By the size of the community

Yes 43.19%
No 56.81%

Yes 42.82%
No 57.18%

Yes 50.41%
No 49.59%

Yes 47.50%
No 52.50%

Yes 67.39%
No 32.61%

500–2500

2500–5000

5000–25,000

25,000–100,000

Over 100,000

the South, which stresses spiritual values more, also gives greater assistance to their teachers in this respect.

Bible Reading. The reading of the Holy Scriptures has been the subject of much state legislation. In most states Bible reading is either permitted, allowed by virtue of silence, or required by law. Actual practice varies as to portions read, who shall read them, scheduling during the school day, and even the number of verses. In allowing or requiring Bible reading the assumption is that the Scriptures are not sectarian. Often the Bible is read as part of a simple opening school ceremony, at school assemblies at chapel services, or homeroom exercises. Some examples of Bible reading practices in public schools follow.

The state of Idaho has on its statute books a law which requires daily reading from the American Standard version of the Bible. The state board of education prepares a list of approved readings from which twelve to twenty verses are to be read without comment.[22] The Idaho state department of education publishes a list of selections containing 418 readings from both Old and New Testaments.[23]

A statement in the "Elementary Curriculum for the Meridian, Mississippi Public Schools" sounds a religious note for the public schools:

"Teaching the Bible is not necessarily religious instruction; it is only a means to this end. . . Children love the stories of the Old and New Testaments because they are true and because they are adaptable to life today. It is not enough to read a passage from the Bible to children; some comment should be made that they may be able to understand its meaning in so far as they are capable . . .

"There should be a definite place on the daily program for the Bible. It should be read often . . . There should be a Bible with large print on the reading table of every room where children can find and use it. Every teacher should have her own copy on her desk."[24]

This program of Scripture reading is not restricted either as to New or Old Testaments, number of verses, or to comment and interpretation by the teacher. Such a plan in many parts of the country would probably receive vigorous opposition on the grounds of sectarian influence. This represents an extreme in Bible reading and may be contrasted with localities which prohibit any reading at all.

Reports from school superintendents indicate variations on the extent to which Bible reading occurs in public schools. They were asked about the type of Bible used and if students who objected were excused. Charts appearing on the following pages show the results of the questions.

The reading of the Bible is practiced by a large number of school systems (41.74%). The South (76.84%) again leads the way with the West reporting the lowest percentage (11.03%).

By far the most popular version of the Bible used in the replying schools is the King James version, employed in 70.65% of the schools. The American Revised Standard version is found in 38.43% and the Roman Catholic Bible in 5.18%. A number of systems use more than one version of the Bible.

Students who do not wish to hear the Bible read are excused in 40.05% of the school systems and required to remain in 59.95%.

Bible Classes. Courses in the Bible constitute another religious influence in public schools. Such classes are taught under varying circumstances. Some school systems employ special teachers while others use regular staff members. In most instances credit toward graduation is given, and in all cases such classes are elective. The following quotation from a school superintendent provides an example of how one southern city conducts its Bible classes:

"We have five full-time teachers of the Bible in the public schools on our staff. Three of them work in the high schools and teach pupils who elect the course which is a one-year course meeting daily and open to any senior high school student. Most of the pupils are either juniors or seniors. In addition to these three, we have two teachers in the elementary schools who teach children in the fifth and sixth grades. These teachers are itinerant teachers and go to the classroom and take over for a thirty-minute period. Children whose parents object to their being in the class are excused to go to the library or office or some other suitable place. There are a few Jews and Baptists and Catholics who do not remain in the room. The salaries of these teachers are paid by the churches and by interested individuals, and the 'Advisory Committee on the Teaching of the Bible in the Public schools' works with the Board of Education in securing funds and in working with the teachers on the curriculum. The teachers are paid through the regular channels of our office, the money being turned into our office and therefore, the expenditure is equal to the income . . . The teachers use a syllabus in the high school course but the basis for the teaching is the Bible itself. Our high school teachers are very competent folks, well trained,

CHART V

Is Bible reading conducted in the schools of your system?

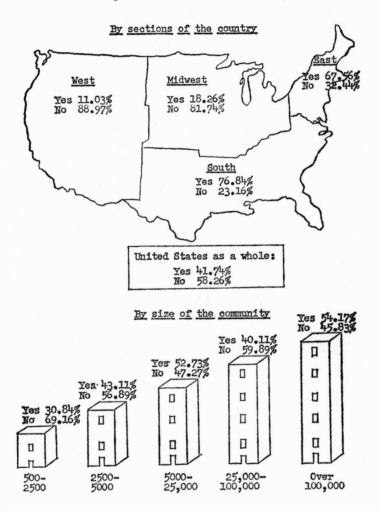

By sections of the country

East
Yes 67.56%
No 32.44%

West
Yes 11.03%
No 88.97%

Midwest
Yes 18.26%
No 81.74%

South
Yes 76.84%
No 23.16%

United States as a whole:
Yes 41.74%
No 58.26%

By size of the community

Yes 30.84%
No 69.16%

Yes 43.11%
No 56.89%

Yes 52.73%
No 47.27%

Yes 40.11%
No 59.89%

Yes 54.17%
No 45.83%

500–2500 2500–5000 5000–25,000 25,000–100,000 Over 100,000

and very enthusiastic people. The children are not forced to take the course, but numbers of them do . . . " [25]

This plan would undoubtedly meet stiff opposition in some sections of the country and of course in the states which prohibit Bible reading would be illegal.

Knoxville, Tennessee, has Bible classes which operate under the following conditions:

"Bible is taught in the Knoxville City junior and senior high schools, with properly certified teachers and credit toward graduation for one-half or one full credit, approved by the State Board of Education.

"Bible teachers are selected and salaries are paid by the Local Ministerial Association." [26]

The Dallas, Texas city school systems allows instruction according to the following regulations:

"1. Minimum number of class periods are, forty periods of 90 minutes, sixty of 60 minutes, or eighty of 45 minutes.

"2. The texts used are the *Bible Study Course, Old Testament*, and *Bible Study Course New Testament*, authorized by the Board of Education.

"3. The teacher must have a minimum of at least a high school education, and sufficient teaching experience or training in Bible to warrant success in teaching a Bible course. Graduation from college is desirable.

"4. There must be a suitable room in which to conduct class work. A small library of reference and supplementary books is necessary for the best work.

"5. A credit course should have a beginning enrollment of not fewer than three students.

"6. Each course is open to students of the ninth, tenth, eleventh, and twelfth grades.

"7. Accurate records of attendance and date of class meeting must be kept.

"8. All students who desire credit must pass an examination held under the auspices of the Board of Education." [27]

These illustrations give some idea of typical programs of Bible classes in public high schools. Classes in the Bible authorized by the public schools, in some cases taught in the school buildings, and offering credit toward graduation must be classed as a significant religious influence in the systems which operate such an enterprise.

Very few schools (4.51%) report regular formal Bible instruction.

Nearly one system in ten throughout the South permits Bible classes while only about one in a hundred in the East has such courses. Of those school systems reporting Bible classes, most (59.55%) do not carry credit and most (64.04%) are not paid for by school funds.

Homeroom Devotional Exercises. The school day in many communities opens with a short worship service conducted within each classroom. Led by students or teachers it may consist of Scripture reading, prayers, devotional talks and hymn singing. Some schools use the public address system for a short service daily. The Houston, Texas, public schools publish a curriculum bulletin which contains a section designed to help teachers prepare effective devotionals. It includes sample programs, Bible selections, representative prayers, religious poems, and other selections appropriate to the occasion.[28]

A number of excerpts from school bulletins show how opening services of worship are used in the public schools.

In Baltimore schools: "Each school, either collectively or in classes, shall be opened by the reading, without comment, of a chapter in the Holy Bible and/or the use of the Lord's Prayer." [29]

The Springfield, Missouri, teachers are urged to "Provide for their pupils such inspirational experiences as prayer, Bible reading, devotional programs, and special religious assemblies, provided that such experiences are non-denominational and are of general interest and appreciation." [30]

In Tulsa, Oklahoma: "Bible reading and prayer are engaged in daily in all schools." [31]

"Many teachers open the day with a brief prayer and reading of the Bible in the clasroom", in the Richmond, Virginia system.[32]

The Montgomery, Alabama public schools use: "Bible reading each day, frequently accompanied by prayer as part of the homeroom procedure.[33]

Teachers in Knoxville, Tennessee, are advised that "Homeroom devotions should be planned and purposeful and should be carried on in a reverent, unhurried manner. The selection should be read with understanding, even if it is necessary for the teacher to do it." [34]

Opening exercises of a religious nature are certain to differ widely in emphasis, length, and depth of spiritual content.

The situation regarding the prevalence of homeroom devotional exercises presents an odd picture. The results for the nation as a whole indicate 33.16% of the schools conduct these services. It is the contrast between the South and East on the one hand and the Midwest and

CHART VI

Are there regular classes in the Bible in the schools of your system?

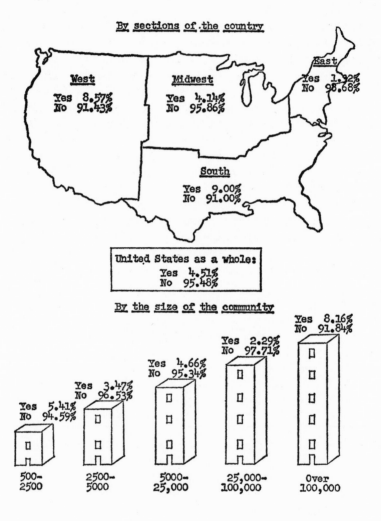

By sections of the country

East
Yes 1.32%
No 98.68%

West
Yes 8.57%
No 91.43%

Midwest
Yes 4.14%
No 95.86%

South
Yes 9.00%
No 91.00%

United States as a whole:
Yes 4.51%
No 95.48%

By the size of the community

Yes 5.41%
No 94.59%
500-2500

Yes 3.47%
No 96.53%
2500-5000

Yes 4.66%
No 95.34%
5000-25,000

Yes 2.29%
No 97.71%
25,000-100,000

Yes 8.16%
No 91.84%
Over 100,000

54

West on the other which is so unusual. In the South 60.53% of the systems have homeroom devotionals in all schools and the East has an even larger percentage (68.33%), whereas the Midwest has only 6.40% and the West only 2.41%. A high correlation exists between the figures on homeroom devotional exercises and those on Bible reading. It is probable that Bible reading is a part of the homeroom devotional or that such services are built around scripture reading.

In the survey, if major questions received affirmative replies, inquiries were then made about certain aspects of the practice. Answers to these contingent questions furnish additional information on details of each program. For example, the number of situations in which both students and teachers conduct homeroom services is a percentage of the combined total for "all schools" and "some schools." This figure (81.45%) indicates it is the most popular method of handling these services in the school systems which do have such exercises. The most extensively used activity is the reading of Scripture (74.39%). Following in popularity are prayer (69.12%), devotional talks (19.59%), and singing of hymns (17.61%).

The use of the public address system to carry devotional exercises into clasrooms is not popular across the nation. (23.45% of the answering school systems use it.)

Units on Religion in Regular Coursework. In course planning, teachers frequently lay out major subdivisions called units. Especially in the fields of social studies, literature, music, and art—religion, particularly its historical and cultural impact, often provides the theme around which such units are organized.

The Indianapolis public schools include units on religion in seventh and eighth grade courses. The approach used is "factual teaching about" procedure. In the words of the introduction to both units: "The public schools may not teach religion, but should and must teach *about* religion and the role it has played and is playing in the development of the way of life of the people of America and of the world." [85] In the seventh grade unit on "Our Religious Heritage" a few samples from the specific objectives point to the nature of the material to be presented:

"To know the origins of our leading religious faiths.

"To know the important part taken in the religious struggle by Martin Luther. Ignatius Loyola, John Calvin, etc.

"To know the faiths of some of the men of early America." [36]

CHART VII

Are homeroom devotional services held in the schools of your system?

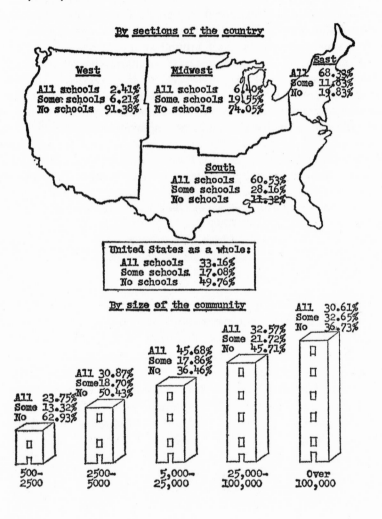

By sections of the country

West
All schools   2.41%
Some schools 6.21%
No schools   91.38%

Midwest
All schools   6.40%
Some schools 19.55%
No schools   74.05%

East
All   68.33%
Some 11.83%
No   19.83%

South
All schools   60.53%
Some schools 28.16%
No schools   11.32%

United States as a whole:
All schools   33.16%
Some schools   17.08%
No schools   49.76%

By size of the community

All   23.75%
Some   13.32%
No   62.93%
500—2500

All   30.87%
Some   18.70%
No   50.43%
2500—5000

All   45.68%
Some   17.86%
No   36.46%
5,000—25,000

All   32.57%
Some   21.72%
No   45.71%
25,000—100,000

All   30.61%
Some   32.65%
No   36.73%
Over 100,000

Typical of the "suggested activities" designed to achieve these goals are the following:

"Discuss colonies founded as a result of religious persecution.

"Find out how religion influenced the making of the calendars.

"Give examples to show how men of early America relied on religion to direct their lives." [67]

An eleven page appendix contains factual material designed to help teachers.

The eighth grade unit focuses attention on the role of religion in the historical development of the United States. In addition it emphasizes the religious climate of the city of Indianapolis, and the appendix includes figures on church membership in the city.

At West High School in Denver, Colorado, the twelfth grade course in "American Problems" contains a unit on "Philosophy and Religious Values." The section headings of the subject content outline give an idea as to the areas to be covered in the unit:

"I. What is religion?

"II. Where do I get a system of values to guide my life?

"III. Why should I be understanding toward the beliefs of others?

"IV. In what do I believe?

"V. What is the relationship between religion, morals, and character?

"VI. What does religion contribute to society?

"VII. What is prayer?

"VIII. What are some of the great stories of religion?

"IX. Why should I have a religion?

"X. What is the place of religious values in my plan of action?" [38]

Tulsa, Oklahoma, uses the religious unit plan in their schools: "In ninth grade civics a unit deals with religion as one of the social foundations of American life. All denominationalism has been carefully avoided but pupils are led to understand the significance of religious life and its effect on both the individual and the nation. Also in tenth grade history one unit, "How Our American Ideals Evolved," deals with the significance of religion in the history of this nation." [39]

The Tulsa approach goes a step further than the incidental reference to religion discussed earlier. Teaching *about* religion through such units is the technique advocated by the American Council on Education and other groups. If such instruction can be handled in a non-denominational way, it holds promise of giving religion a place in the curriculum without teaching sectarianism.

The response of superintendents to the questionnaire reveals the extent of teaching *about* religion and the popularity of organized units on religion.

Materials to assist in teaching *about* religion are provided in 76.06% of the communities polled. Most of this material appears to have been developed outside of the local school system.

The answers to the inquiry which sought to determine the popularity of regular organized units dealing with the influence of religion on past and present culture, showed that in 80.60% of the elementary schools questioned there was no such program. An interesting variation can be seen in cities of over 100,000 population which report 43.90% of elementary grades have such units. In social studies area in secondary schools, the lowest figure comes from ninth grade social studies, 9.66%, while world history provides the highest, 51.53%. About one-third (38.02%) of the school systems use this type of unit in the teaching of literature, with the Midwest reporting a top figure of 60.79%.

Religious References in Textbooks. Most educational authorities, whether they agree with the principle or not, recognize that much of the teaching in the present-day American school depends on a textbok as the basic source of information. The courses in which religion is an instrinsic part, such as social studies, literature, art, music, and others, use texts which contain references to religion. In a study conducted at Yale University an attempt was made to determine quantitatively the references to religious subjects in textbooks used in the public schools of Missouri. It is not known exactly how representative the sample taken was of texts throughout American schools, although it would be reasonable to suppose that in general it reflects the practices of the majority of textbook writers and publishers. More than 113 textbooks from twenty different publishing houses were examined[40] and the following facts found:

Of the 113 textbooks examined, 106 contained some reference to religion.[41]

The word "religion" or "religious" was used 628 times.

There were 639 references to the various kinds of religion, with Christianity receiving 336 references.

Church as it relates to Christianity was referred to 1,421 times.

Prayer and the act of prayer was mentioned 435 times.

There were 1,609 references to groups or classes of persons related to religious fellowships.

Life after death was referred to 485 times.

CHART VIII

Does your school system provide materials to classroom teachers to help in teaching about religion?

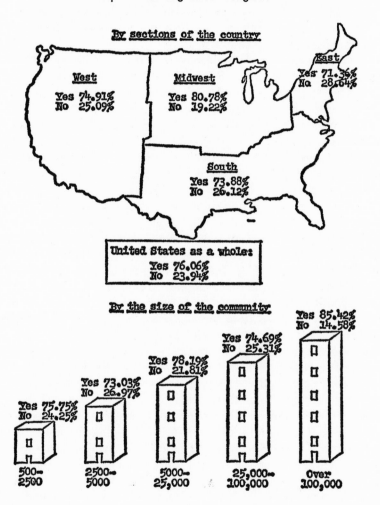

By sections of the country

East
Yes 71.36%
No 28.64%

West
Yes 74.91%
No 25.09%

Midwest
Yes 80.78%
No 19.22%

South
Yes 73.88%
No 26.12%

United States as a whole:
Yes 76.06%
No 23.94%

By the size of the community

Yes 85.42%
No 14.58%

Yes 74.69%
No 25.31%

Yes 78.19%
No 21.81%

Yes 73.03%
No 26.97%

Yes 75.75%
No 24.25%

500—
2500

2500—
5000

5000—
25,000

25,000—
100,000

Over
100,000

59

Some interesting conclusions were drawn about the trends of religious reference in textbooks. Among these were:

1. The number and volume of religious references increases with
advancing school grades.

2. The concepts used are inadequately described, defined, and
interpreted. Apparently the students are expected to bring religious
background to their textbook reading.

3. It is possible to deal objectively and informatively with controversial religious matters. Some of the textbooks do so.

4. The closer we get to textbook descriptions of present day life and
literature the fewer religious references there are.[42]

The author of the study seems to feel that while there are many
references to religion in textbooks, the writers can improve their
efforts in this respect. Through the use of clearer definitions and
descriptions of terms, increased references in lower grade texts, and
greater emphasis on the role of religion in present-day affairs, the
students can receive a fuller understanding of the relation of religion
and culture.

Inclusion of religious subjects in study material is a sensitive subject
in some localities. Shakespeare's *Merchant of Venice* was protested
as being anti-Semitic by Jews in New York, while in Buffalo it is
banned from the regular curriculum.[43] In other cities textbooks which
are offensive to Protestants or Catholics have been protested and
occasionally dropped from the approved list because of sectarian opposition. It is easy to agree with Justice Jackson when he says: "But
how one can teach, with satisfaction or even with justice to all faiths,
such subjects as the story of the Reformation, the Inquisition, or even
the New England effort to found 'a Church with a Bishop and a State
without a King,' is more than I know . . . "[44]

Any move to eliminate all references to religion in textbooks simply
because it is a controversial subject is not facing the issue. As Pflug
maintains, it is possible to treat religion objectively as some texts have
done. The aim must be to have such treatment in all public school
textbooks. While this is a very difficult task, publishing houses
need to be especially critical of biased references to religion in any
book designed for use in the schools.

Extra-Courricular Activities. The tax-supported schools are prohibited by law from engaging in any promotion of sectarian religion,
in both curricular and extra-curricular activities. Use of school
property for denominational club meetings such as Luther League,

Newman clubs, and others is not condoned in most localities. However, a number of schools undoubtedly post notices of meetings for these organizations on school bulletin boards. Several extra-curricular activities, while not denominational in character, do emphasize spiritual values. For example, the Hi-Y clubs and Y-Teens have for many years given a high place to religion and engage in prayers and devotional exercises during meetings. Bible study clubs form part of the extra-curricular programs of some public schools. Participation in such welfare drives as the Junior Red Cross may be motivated by religious considerations. Much of the music sung by school choirs has a spiritual theme. Student participation in assemblies which have a religious tone also constitutes an influence in the public schools. The Knoxville, Tennessee, school system urges that: "Those in charge of extra-curricular groups should be constantly aware of opportunities for training in moral and spiritual values." [45] How much influence results from the extra-curricular activities depends on the attitude of the school administrator and on the approach of the faculty sponsor. If these two individuals are anxious to foster religious values through the work of the extra-curricular program, its impact will probably be important.

The amount and nature of religious influence found in the curriculum of American public schools runs the gamut from incidental mention of religious subjects in the classroom to Bible classes and planned units on religion. In any of these activities the old educational maxim: "It's what happens in the classroom that counts" still holds. The individual teacher largely controls the degree of religious influence.

CHAPTER V

NON-CLASS ACTIVITIES AND RELIGIOUS INFLUENCE

Non-curricular activities sponsored by the school, apart from regular academic offerings, provide a significant portion of the educational process and often have a profound effect on the thinking and behavior of students. The nature and type of these activities indicate to the student the individual school's religious attitude. Religious activities can range from excusing pupils from school to observe special holy days to conducting a full fledged religious service in the school building. A number of these outside activities are described and analyzed below.

Baccalaureate Service. For some students the only time they will attend a religious service is during the baccalaureate of their high school class. This ceremony cannot be considered a great influence on the students, but it is one method through which religion is brought into the school. The typical service includes invocation, Scripture, prayer, hymn singing, sacred music, sermon, and benediction. Usually the honor of delivering the baccalaureate sermon is passed from one minister to another in the community. Several denominations are nearly always represented on the platform for such an event.

Protests against such a religious service sponsored by the public schools are heard from time to time. They often come from the Roman Catholic clergy and occasionally from some branches of the Lutheran Church. Because of the somewhat controversial nature of this ceremony and the disagreement it has aroused, the superintendents were asked in the survey to report the situation in their localities.

The traditional Baccalaureate service appears to be firmly entrenched as a part of high school graduation activities in the American school system. Throughout the nation 86.84% of the public schools conduct such exercises. Only in the East where 68.13% use it, does its widespread popularity seem in danger. The larger the town the less likelihood of Baccalaureate activities being found. The answers to contingent questions point out some interesting practices. Nearly all schools which have these services hold them on school property and not in churches (85.63%). Approximately two-thirds of the systems (67.43%) make Baccalaureate a voluntary affair. Relatively small protest has been made over this activity (10.33%). A significant comparison can be made between the amount of protest in the East (23.77%) and the South (2.61%). Most localities feel this is a tradition and therefore in only 9.99% of the replying school systems is a vote of the seniors taken on whether or not to hold Baccalaureate services. Very few schools (2.99%) plan to discontinue the use of this activity.

Regular Chapel Exercises. Some schools hold non-denominational religious services regularly, usually each week. The following quotation illustrates how one school handles its chapel services: "The school is divided into groups. . . The older children, about 300 in the sixth and seventh grades, meet once a week in a chapel service. The choral-speaking choir presents songs and recitations and the children are taught the meaning of the words. Each child has a copy of the New Testament and a passage from it is read each week." [1]

New Holland, Michigan schools have during the past several years held daily chapel exercises. In the high school these devotionals last twenty-five minutes with students participating and often conducting the entire program. Junior high and elementary grades hold worship in their classrooms daily with Bible reading and prayer.[2] This regular worship on school property during school time might be questioned on legal grounds in some states for there is certainly a religious influence in the schools as a result of the custom.

Again, in the matter of regular chapel exercises, the survey reveals sectional differences. From the low in the West (1.35%) the percentage of school systems employing this procedure rises to a high in the South of 70.86% of the replying schools. The national figure was found to be 22.07%.

Contingent question replies point up some other interesting facts. Of the school systems which have chapel exercises, 70.49% require the students to attend. The most popular method of handling these services combines the efforts of both teachers and students (82.16%). Such activities are held weekly by 43.09% of the schools, monthly by 22.93%, and daily by 5.73%.

Assembly Procedures Involving Religion. The school assembly, as distinct from the chapel exercise which is purely devotional in nature, is usually not called for religious reasons and is hence a secular affair. Many school systems take advantage of the gathering of the

CHART IX

Are baccalaureate services conducted in connection with high school graduation?

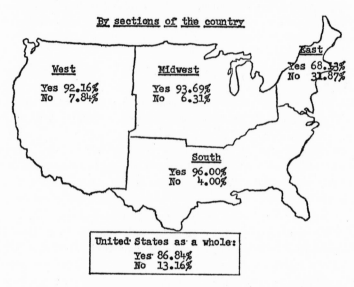

By sections of the country

West
Yes 92.16%
No 7.84%

Midwest
Yes 93.69%
No 6.31%

East
Yes 68.13%
No 31.87%

South
Yes 96.00%
No 4.00%

United States as a whole:
Yes 86.84%
No 13.16%

By size of the community

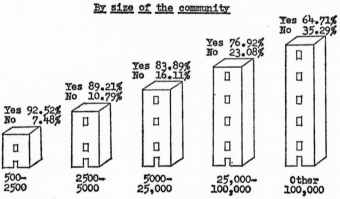

Yes 92.52%
No 7.48%

Yes 89.21%
No 10.79%

Yes 83.89%
No 16.11%

Yes 76.92%
No 23.08%

Yes 64.71%
No 35.29%

500–
2500

2500–
5000

5000–
25,000

25,000–
100,000

Other
100,000

whole student body to include an aspect of worship in the program, such as the singing of a hymn, a prayer, or Bible reading. The following practices are examples:

The Board of Education of Pittsburgh, Pennsylvania public schools advises staff members that "The reverent reading of the Bible at assemblies, the saying of the Lord's Prayer with bowed heads, and the singing of hymns of praise create an atmosphere of religious devotion and of praise. At times such as these on special occasions, many religious practices common to the group can be used." [3]

In Tulsa "All assemblies open with rituals that are inspiring and deeply religious without denominationalism, and the content of most assemblies emphasizes patriotic and spiritual values." [4]

Unless the inclusion of religious acts in assembly programs is done in a careful and understanding way such practices may become a meaningless rote performance and do more harm than good in developing spiritual values. If this part of school assemblies is executed with reverence by all concerned, the religious influence could be strong.

Observance of Religious Holidays. Many public schools make a place in their schedules for programs celebrating religious holidays. The commemoration of Christmas is nearly universal in American schools although some sharp disagreements have resulted from the custom. The typical Christmas assembly will usually include a play presenting some aspect of the story of Christ's birth, Scripture reading, the singing of carols, and solo and choir selections of a seasonal tone. Easter is also widely celebrated by special observances.

The Tulsa schools teach moral and spiritual values, "through dramatizations of stories at Thanksgiving, Christmas and Easter . . ." [5]
In Atlanta, "Some schools take entire student bodies into a neighboring church for special Christmas and other services." - [6]

In Portland they: ". . . also use such devices as Christmas programs, Thanksgiving programs, and Easter assemblies to teach certain lessons relating to the areas of moral and spiritual values to our students." [7]

In some communities especially with large Jewish populations, the observance of Christmas is criticized as a sectarian practice in the public schools.

The compromise solution of celebrating both the Christian holiday and the Jewish holiday, Hanukkah, which comes near Christmas has been suggested. Such an attempt is reported by the Richmond paper: "In the Christmas Pageant this year, John Marshall High

CHART X

Is there any type of regular chapel exercise held in the schools of your system?

By sections of the country

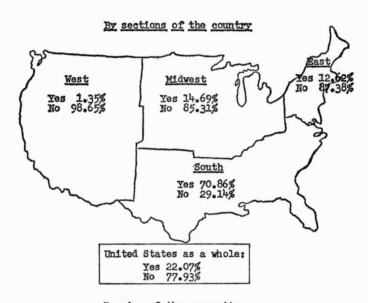

West
Yes 1.35%
No 98.65%

Midwest
Yes 14.69%
No 85.31%

East
Yes 12.62%
No 87.38%

South
Yes 70.86%
No 29.14%

United States as a whole:
Yes 22.07%
No 77.93%

By size of the community

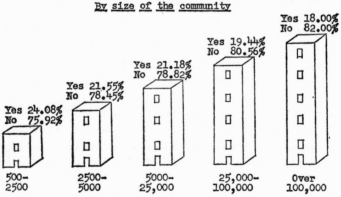

Yes 24.08%
No 75.92%

Yes 21.55%
No 78.45%

Yes 21.18%
No 78.82%

Yes 19.44%
No 80.56%

Yes 18.00%
No 82.00%

500– 2500

2500– 5000

5000– 25,000

25,000– 100,000

Over 100,000

66

School will show how the holiday evolved from the Jewish celebration of Hanukkah." [8]   This procedure has not had much support from Jewish groups as they feel neither holiday should be commemorated in public schools.   The observance of Christmas and other religious holidays can be classified as significant religious influence in the public schools, but in some cases sectarian conflict has marred the atmosphere of the occasion.

Survey results show, not surprisingly, that the most popular religious holidays are Christmas (87.92%), Thanksgiving (76.75%), and Easter (57.82%).   The important thing to remember is that these holidays are not only observed by a vacation but by school activities which commemorate them in one way or another.

Excusing Students For Religious Holidays of Their Faiths.   It has become a common practice in public schools to excuse children for special religious celebrations.   This custom not only allows the pupils to attend the worship but indicates that the schools wish to encourage students in their chosen religion.   An example of how some school systems treat the problem of "Holy Day excuses" is the policy in Denver, Colorado, where "there are certain days during the school year when children of several faiths may be excused from school by parent request.   Catholic high school students may attend a retreat in the spring which lasts for two or three days, if they bring to their teacher a card from their pastor with their parent's signature. Children of the Bahai faith are excused from school at the request of parents on ten holy days, and Jewish children on fifteen holy days during the year." [9]

The actual religious influence on the students resulting from a knowledge that the school excuses them to attend holy day celebration may be small, but the realization that the school sanctions efforts of students to follow religious beliefs may have effect.

According to survey results 70.71% of the nation's school systems excuse students to take part in special religious holidays, not including Christmas, Thanksgiving, and Easter.   The East is most likely to do this (85.37%) and the South least apt to (53.67%).

Lunchtime Blessing.   A short non-denominational grace is offered before the noon meal in some school cafeterias.   This custom prevails in Montgomery, Alabama; Richmond, Virginia; and Houston, Texas. According to the *Richmond Times-Dispatch*, "A blessing is given during each lunch period in the cafeteria and the children consider it a privilege to be selected to give the prayer." [10]   In Houston, "In some

CHART XI

Are religious holidays observed by any kind of activities in the schools of your system?

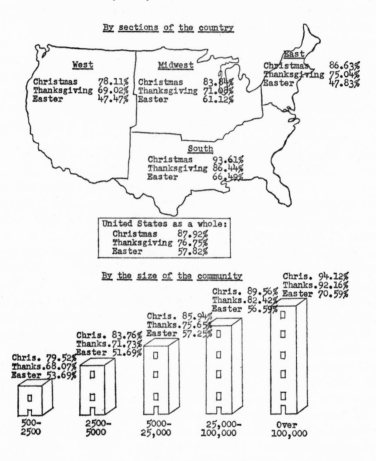

By sections of the country

West
Christmas   78.11%
Thanksgiving   69.02%
Easter   47.47%

Midwest
Christmas   83.84%
Thanksgiving   71.08%
Easter   61.12%

East
Christmas   86.63%
Thanksgiving   75.04%
Easter   47.83%

South
Christmas   93.61%
Thanksgiving   86.44%
Easter   66.49%

United States as a whole:
Christmas   87.92%
Thanksgiving   76.75%
Easter   57.82%

By the size of the community

500-2500
Chris. 79.52%
Thanks. 68.07%
Easter 53.69%

2500-5000
Chris. 83.76%
Thanks. 71.73%
Easter 51.69%

5000-25,000
Chris. 85.94%
Thanks. 75.65%
Easter 57.25%

25,000-100,000
Chris. 89.56%
Thanks. 82.42%
Easter 56.59%

Over 100,000
Chris. 94.12%
Thanks. 92.16%
Easter 70.59%

schools, particularly elementary schools, the devotional exercise comes at the lunch period." [11] If such a prayer is spoken in a reverent manner, it may encourage or strengthen similar family observances. If it is rattled off in a haphazard manner with a great deal of noise in the background, it could become more ridiculous than worshipful.

The practice of providing for a grace before lunch in the school lunchroom is found in about one-third of the school systems. The smallest combined total for two categories, "all schools" and "varies with each school in the system", is 14.23% in the West. The largest total (66.05%) is found in the South. Of the schools which make provision for a blessing, silent prayer is found in 46.93% of them. Of types of spoken prayers, those of students (54.20%) are most popular, with those of teachers a poor second (28.96%). Written prayers on tables or lunchroom walls have little support (4.71%)

Selection of Teachers With Religious Convictions. While it is contrary to practice, custom, and law in many areas of the country to inquire into the denomination of a prospective teacher, many school officials do require that the instructors in their schools believe in some religion. Typical of those states which bar questions on religion is Minnesota which, on the basis of a fair employment practices law, forbids asking teachers about their race or religion. The laws of nine states have sections requiring teachers to be of good moral character. [12]

Official guidelines for the elementary curriculum for the Meridian, Mississippi public schools state that "The teacher must have an abiding faith in God and be able to adapt His teachings to life today . . . She should be so filled with the Spirit of Christ that through her daily Christian living she may see Jesus live in her own pupils." [13] This is not a criterion for hiring new teachers, but the fact that such a direct statement is part of an accepted curriculum guide points to the likelihood of a similar point of view in connection with selection of new personnel.

A less definite policy was outlined by Superintendent Willett of Richmond, Virginia, when he said: "It is of first importance to have the finest persons to shape the character of future generations. In selecting a teacher denomination never enters the picture but she should have a belief in a power greater than man, a stable character and a good personality." [14]

No explicit requirement is made for new teachers in the Atlanta, Georgia school system, but "The community takes great pride in the fact that all of the school officials and most of the principals, teachers

CHART XII

Are students excused to observe special religious holidays?
(Excluding Christmas, Easter, and Thanksgiving)

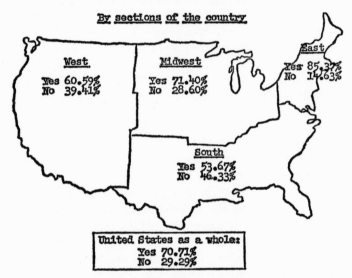

By sections of the country

West
Yes 60.59%
No 39.41%

Midwest
Yes 71.40%
No 28.60%

East
Yes 85.37%
No 14.63%

South
Yes 53.67%
No 46.33%

United States as a whole:
Yes 70.71%
No 29.29%

By the size of the community

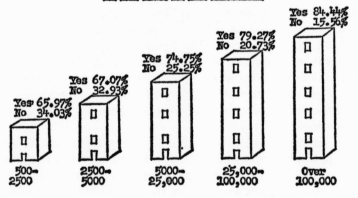

Yes 65.97%
No 34.03%

Yes 67.07%
No 32.93%

Yes 74.75%
No 25.25%

Yes 79.27%
No 20.73%

Yes 84.44%
No 15.56%

500-
2500

2500-
5000

5000-
25,000

25,000-
100,000

Over
100,000

and employees occupy positions of leadership in their respective churches." [15]

A consecrated and sincerely religious teacher can be one of the greatest religious influences in the public schools. Many students can testify that the example and precept of a beloved teacher has had tremendous religious effect on pupils. There are some significant dangers involved in giving too much emphasis to the religious beliefs of teachers. Some hiring officials may place religious conformity ahead of teaching ability and select persons of sincere belief who lack the ability to instruct children. Another difficulty arises when a hiring officer tends to favor his own denomination, or the Protestant, Catholic, or Jewish group to which he belongs. A third drawback involves the hiring of persons who are so firm in their own beliefs that not only are they unable to see other points of view but they try to proselyte students to their particular religious affiliation.

Miscellaneous Regional Religious Practices. There are several influences which are peculiar to certain cities, states, or regions of the country. These are consolidated under a single section since they are not widely used.

1. Display of the Ten Commandments in Classrooms: Three states use this device as a technique to inculcate in the students a knowledge of and respect for these spiritual laws of the Old Testament. In Minnesota an attorney general's opinion in 1952 permits the display of the Ten Commandments in public school classrooms. [16] The Mississippi Educational Code requires instruction in the Ten Commandments. [17] The North Dakota school laws state "It shall be the duty of the School Board, Board of Trustees, or Board of Education of every school district . . . to display a placard containing the Ten Commandments of the Christian religion [sic] in a conspicuous place in every school room, classroom or other place in said school where classes convene for instruction." [18] How much effect such display has on the religious life of the pupils is impossible to gauge. The writer attended public school in North Dakota and clearly remembers seeing framed reproductions of the Ten Commandments in his classrooms. As far as he can recall no specific reference to them was made by the teachers, but the fact that the school believed the Commandments important enough to place in each classroom did impress him.

2. Keeping Records of Sunday School Attendance: This practice is mentioned because one large Southern city, Birmingham, does make it a point to keep rather comprehensive records on the number

CHART XIII

In lunchrooms of the schools in your system is there provision
for prayer before meals?

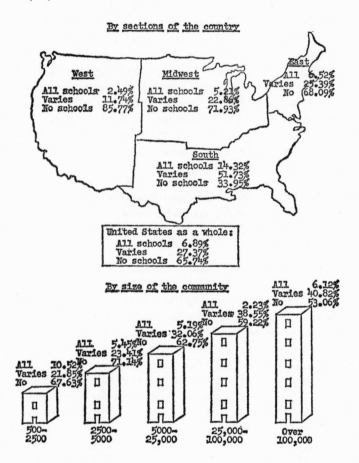

By sections of the country

East
All   6.52%
Varies   25.39%
No   68.09%

West
All schools   2.49%
Varies   11.74%
No schools   85.77%

Midwest
All schools   5.21%
Varies   22.86%
No schools   71.93%

South
All schools   14.32%
Varies   51.73%
No schools   33.95%

United States as a whole:
All schools   6.89%
Varies   27.37%
No schools   65.74%

By size of the community

All   6.12%
Varies   40.82%
No   53.06%

All   2.23%
Varies   38.55%
No   59.22%

All   5.19%
Varies   32.06%
No   62.75%

All   5.45%
Varies   23.41%
No   71.14%

All   10.52%
Varies   21.85%
No   67.63%

500-   2500-   5000-   25,000-   Over
2500   5000   25,000   100,000   100,000

of students attending the Sunday schools of the city. The system is operated in the following fashion: Each school is required to turn in a report on the students who said they went to Sunday School for each of the four Sundays preceding Easter. The actual number who claim to have gone is broken down into denominational groups. Added importance and emphasis may be given to the custom of Sunday school attendance because the schools keep track of who goes and who does not. On the other hand, attending Sunday School merely to avoid admitting non-attendance, might be considered questionable motivation. The propriety of having a school system check on such attendance may be debatable.

3. Mormon "Seminaries": The Church of Jesus Christ of Latter-day Saints has developed the policy of giving instruction to high schoo! students of Mormon belief. The church believes "firmly in a separation of Church and State," [19] but also holds that education is not complete without religion. Because of the concise way Dr. William E. Barrett described the program, his letter to the writer will be quoted here at some length:

"It is our practice to build independent schools adjacent to public high schools and to offer courses in Old and New Testament studies and in the history and doctrine of the Church taught by privately employed teachers who have academic standards at least comparable and frequently superior to those of the teachers in the high school. This independent school is called a "Seminary" and is supported solely by the Church.

"Where released time can be obtained during various hours of the day, students are excused from the public high school to attend the Seminary . . . These classes meet one hour a day every day the public high school is in session. Studies in Old and New Testament, which are considered non-sectarian, are given credit on transfer to the high school and are classified as electives in compiling student credits.

"In areas where released time is not available or where the number of LDS students in a high school does not justify a full daytime program, classes are held at an hour prior to the commencement of the regular school day. These classes are also taught on a high scholastic level by teachers holding college degrees. At the present time we have approximately 120 full-time Seminaries, and 425 part-time Seminaries or Seminaries which meet students at an hour prior to the regular school day . . . Current enrollment is approximately 40,000 students in the Seminaries . . ." [20]

This extensive program of religious training to supplement sectarian education shows the real concern of the Mormon Church in this area. It is reasonable to assume that those Mormon students in public high schools who attend the "seminaries" receive important religious influence from such practice.

*   *   *

In reviewing the religious influence of non-curricular activities it can be seen that a few practices are nearly always found while others are used very infrequently. The baccalaureate service remains popular and, despite sporadic protests, indications point to its continuanace. Regular chapel services are the exception rather than the rule in the West, Midwest, and East, but are widely used in the South. The Christian holidays of Christmas and Easter, as well as Thanksgiving, are celebrated by school activities in the majority of American schools and excusing students for the observation of special religious holidays is a common practice. The custom of providing for prayers before meals in school lunchrooms is not found to be a great extent in any part of the nation.

The section of the country has much to do with the prevalence of certain religious activities. The South rates at or near the top in the percentage of schools reporting religious activity in non-curricular areas.

CHAPTER VI

THE RELEASED TIME PROGRAM

From its beginning in 1913, released time has caught the imagination of many religious and educational leaders. The plan is given several names—released time, excused time, dismissed time, or weekday religious training—but all refer to essentially the same practice. The basis for such a plan is the desire of some churches to give their children additional sectarian instruction. The Sunday schools, it is felt, have not done a satisfactory job, so the released time program has evolved to supplement their efforts. The following characteristics are typical:

1. No public school funds are used to support the program.
2. No coercion is used by the teachers or school officials to obtain attendance.
3. Classes are held in churches or other privately owned buildings.
4. The consent of the parents is required in writing before the children are released.
5. Classes are taught by ministers or other persons not on the public school payroll.
6. Students are excused one hour each week for such instruction.
7. Attendance records are kept by the released time instructors and given to school officials.
8. Sectarian doctrine is taught in the classes.
9. Not all denominations participate in the program.
10. Occasionally the Protestant denominations cooperate in holding general Protestant released time instruction.
11. Students who do not participate are required to remain in classrooms or study halls. Sometimes a program of character education is planned, other times assignments from coursework are studied. Individual school systems place various restrictions on the operation of released time plans as the local situation demands.

The success of the released time approach has been the subject of disagreement between proponents and opponents. Arguments favoring released time and those opposing it can be found in many sources;

therefore, they will be only briefly noted here. The supporters of released time programs give the following as their reasons:

1. Religious instruction can help prevent and cure the low state of morals among young people.

2. One hour a week in Sunday School does not allow sufficient time for adequate religious teaching.

3. The child should identify religion as a weekday idea rather than simply a Sunday ritual.

4. Children who do not go to church are often enrolled in weekday religious instruction.

5. Released time study supplements the secular program received in schools and gives a complete education.

6. It avoids the controversy of the curricular approaches since it is not held under the auspices of the school.

7. It promotes inter-faith understanding when children realize their classmates also go to the released time instruction.

8. It indicates that the school feels religion is important when it cooperates with church authorities in setting up the weekday religious education program.

9. No child is forced to go against his or her parents' wishes, thus making all attendance voluntary.

10. The Supreme Court has approved released time programs when they are not held on school property.

Against these major points for weekday religious instruction those who disagree maintain:

1. The additional hour per week in church school does not allow for much in the way of instruction even if the time going and coming were not considered.

2. The education of the child is already too short and the subtracting of another hour per week should not be allowed.

3. The level of church school education including curricula, facilities and training of teachers is usually low.

4. No satisfactory solution has been discovered to the problem of what to do with those who do not attend classes at the churches.

5. The legal question still exists since the Court was closely divided (five to four) on constitutionality and could easily reverse itself in another case.

6. Religious differences among children are made more noticeable, thus encouraging divisiveness.

7. Coercion exists when students who stay away are made to do distasteful or dull tasks and is also exerted by the fact that children hate to be different from their fellows.

8. It is merely the opening end of a wedge, the ultimate goal being religious education on school time and on school property.

9. The hour taken by released time could easily be made available by a two-hour Sunday school session, a class on Saturday mornings, or other periods without taking school time.

10. Released time is a devisive force in the community.

11. The children who go are those who already have a religious background. Students who need such training do not receive it through this plan.

Ineffective program management invites criticism. Where programs are efficiently organized with well trained teachers and solid support from the churches, criticism appears to be minimal. Fault could easily be found with any poorly planned released time program.

Most of the support for the plan comes from religious groups which have a stake in released time instruction. The National Council of Churches considers the movement so important that it has established a separate Department of Weekday Religious Education to stimulate and coordinate efforts to spread and improve the system.

According to a prominent Catholic writer, the Roman Catholic Church favors the plan: "This program [released time] is primarily of concern to Protestants though I believe, most Catholics endorse it heartily and in many communities Catholics utilize it and cooperate heartily in its administration." [1]

Leo Pfeffer, a close student of released time, does not feel it is too much to say that "the Catholic Church today is the most vigorous and passionate defender of the released-time principle." [2]

Many Protestant groups look with favor on weekday religious training. Missouri Synod Lutherans feel that this means "provides additional time for Christian education." [3] Methodists also favor the plan and "commend to our churches the importance of using through-the-week opportunities for Christian teaching to supplement the work of the church school . . . We recognize the advisability of working with like-minded groups whenever possible in developing and strengthening a system of weekday religious education adequate to its great opportunities." [4]

In a recent official statement the Presbyterian Church in the U.S.A. suggests nine provisions to insure sound and effective programs. [5] The

Mormon Church also endorses weekday religious education in the fullest measure and conducts a program involving 40,000 public school students.[6]

Opposition to the released time idea of religious training is not difficult to locate. Some church groups take strong exception to those who favor it. The American Lutheran Church cautions that "A too-ready and uncritical acceptance of the 'released time' method of giving religious instruction should be avoided. Precaution should be taken that the 'released time' program does not rely upon the 'compulsory attendance' powers of the schools. The church prefers to invite and to persuade rather than to compel, attendance at its religious education curricula."[7]

The Jewish viewpoint is also unfavorable to weekday religious training although they sometimes participate as a sort of self-defense against criticism from other groups.[8]

Opposition to the plan has made some very strange bedfellows. Two such persons are the Reverend Clyde L. Hay and Dr. V. T. Thayer. The Reverend Mr. Hay, for many years on the Sunday School department of the Methodist Episcopal Church, has this to say: "Furthermore, the record of over thirty-five years makes it seem unlikely that the released-time program is in any vital way bridging the chasm between the religiously illiterate portion of our population and those under religious instruction."[9]

Dr. Vivian T. Thayer, connected with the Ethical Culture Society of New York City, has concluded that released time programs are both illegal and unwise "because they represent the efforts of organized pressure groups to use the authority and the prestige of the school in order to conduct classes on school time and in a subject which the law forbids the school itself to teach."[10]

The extent and nature of released time programs have been the subjects of investigation on several occasions. The U.S. Office of Education conducted a poll in 1932 to determine how extensive released time had become in the nation's schools. Replies received from 2,043 cities showed that 218 communities in thirty-five states were employing the released time technique for religious instruction.[11] In 1940 the United States Office of Education again examined the week-day religious instruction of the country's schools. Of the 3,790 replies received, 3,063 school systems had never used the plan; 488 were using it in one form or another; 113 had discontinued the practice; and 126 intended to put such a program into operation.[12]

The McCollum decision early in 1948 had cast doubt on the legality of released time programs in general and those which were conducted on school property in particular. In order to answer some of the questions then being raised, the Research Division of the National Education Association undertook an extensive investigation. In 1948 questionnaires were sent to 5,100 local superintendents of schools in the United States and its territories. Returns were received from 2,639 school authorities, thus giving a 52% reply to the questionnaire. Of the respondents, 1,621 reported they had never atempted any week-day religious instruction, 310 said they formerly used such a plan but had dropped it, and 708 were operating programs in one form or another.[13] These figures in percentages show 73.2% of the replying schools had no plan and 26.8% were using some type of released time. Information received from the survey carried on by the writer indicates further growth. He finds that twelve years after the N.E.A. research was completed, 29.66% of the school systems engage in released time cooperation with churches of the community.

An examination of these survey results reveals significant patterns of development. First, in comparing the results of the United States Office of Education surveys of 1932 and 1940 with figures from the National Education Association study of 1948, a sizeable increase in week-day religious education is evident. In 1932, only 10.7% of the cities surveyed were using released time. By 1940 the figure had risen to 12.8, but in 1948, 26.8 of the responding officials stated that their systems engaged in such a program. In 1960 the number stood at 29.66% of reporting systems cooperating in a released time agreement.

Another interesting fact brought out by the N.E.A. survey was the relationship of the size of the city with the likelihood that it will have released time. In general, the larger the city, the greater the probability exists that its schools have week-day religious training. Cities of lesser size had lower percentages which declined in direct proportion to the smaller population.

Similar findings appear in the results of the school survey conducted by the writer.

Of the replying school officials 29.66% report a released time arrangement in cooperation with local churches. Sectional differences show a rather unusual pattern with the East showing 44.46% of the school systems engaging in such a program and the South only 10.74%.

In 28.38% of the communities only the Roman Catholics provide such instruction and in 22.19% only the Protestants furnish it. Both groups offer released time teaching in 39.97% of the localities. An

CHART XIV

Does your school system cooperate in a program of released time religious instruction?

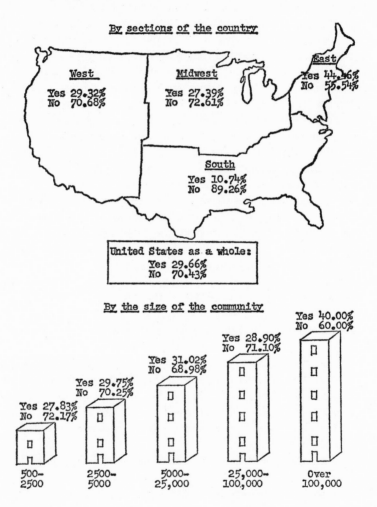

By sections of the country

West
Yes 29.32%
No 70.68%

Midwest
Yes 27.39%
No 72.61%

East
Yes 44.46%
No 55.54%

South
Yes 10.74%
No 89.26%

United States as a whole:
Yes 29.66%
No 70.43%

By the size of the community

Yes 27.83%
No 72.17%

Yes 29.75%
No 70.25%

Yes 31.02%
No 68.98%

Yes 28.90%
No 71.10%

Yes 40.00%
No 60.00%

500– 2500   2500– 5000   5000– 25,000   25,000– 100,000   Over 100,000

80

interesting sidelight in the South points up the fact that 76.92% of the towns and cities have only Protestant released time classes. The Jewish faith makes up only a small proportion of the total. This could be accounted for by the small percentage of the population which is Jewish and the opposition of Jewish groups to the released time concept.

The most popular amount of time given up for religious instruction is a one hour period each week (50.57%). A thirty minute period weekly is allowed in 16.96% of the communities. A combination of time periods depending on the wishes of the groups involved is given in 19.43% of the localities.

The physical facilities used for released time instruction indicates a somewhat strange pattern in the light of the McCollum and Zorach decisions. In 12.72% of the school systems the classes are held on public premises. The South conducts a large proportion of such classes (64.10%) in school buildings. Nationally the churches furnish most of the classrooms (78.79%), while only 4.24% of the communities use private homes.

The levels most frequently selected for released time instruction are grades four, five, and six, but all elementary and secondary grades are extensively utilized. In the Midwest the eighth, ninth and tenth grades are most commonly favored for this purpose.

The released time approach to religious training does not appear to offer an acceptable answer to the majority of school systems. Here, as in other aspects of public school relationship with religion, individual situations vary widely. Much depends on the strength and vitality of local churches and the energy and desire of clergymen and school administrators. The worthiness of released time is largely dependent on the quality of the program, particularly the instruction.

It is difficult to predict the future of released time. In many communities efforts are being made to upgrade the level of instruction through better trained teachers. Curriculum materials have become more plentiful and are of considerably higher quality. Whether these improvements will be instrumental in overcoming objections to the program, only time can tell.

CHART XV

If you do have released time instruction—where are the classes held?

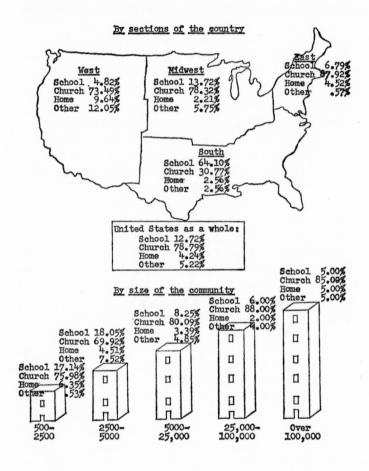

By sections of the country

East
School 6.79%
Church 87.92%
Home 4.52%
Other .57%

West
School 4.82%
Church 73.49%
Home 9.64%
Other 12.05%

Midwest
School 13.72%
Church 78.32%
Home 2.21%
Other 5.75%

South
School 64.10%
Church 30.77%
Home 2.56%
Other 2.56%

United States as a whole:
School 12.72%
Church 78.79%
Home 4.24%
Other 5.22%

By size of the community

School 17.14%
Church 75.98%
Home 6.35%
Other .53%

School 18.05%
Church 69.92%
Home 4.51%
Other 7.52%

School 8.25%
Church 80.09%
Home 3.39%
Other 4.85%

School 6.00%
Church 88.00%
Home 2.00%
Other 4.00%

School 5.00%
Church 85.00%
Home 5.00%
Other 5.00%

500–2500 2500–5000 5000–25,000 25,000–100,000 Over 100,000

CHAPTER VII

RELIGIOUS GROUPS AND THE PUBLIC SCHOOLS

As separation of church and state has become a fixed principle, religious groups and the public educational system have not had a close relationship. Whenever purely religious organizations operate in conjunction with the schools, controversy threatens from real or imagined dangers of sectarian influences.

The problem of public education and religious groups is most potent where population is highly heterogeneous in church affiliation. Communities largely of one faith have least friction, as illustrated by the amount of religious influence in Southern schools where Protestantism is predominant.

Distribution of Religious Literature and Gideon Bibles. Although a number of states have laws prohibiting this practice, in a few instances public schools have used their facilities to pass out denominational literature. In 1952 the New Mexico Supreme Court prohibited the dissemination of sectarian pamphlets through the public schools in a case involving the Presbyterian Church.[1]

The main effort to distribute religious literature in the schools is carried on by the Gideon Society. Since their initial work of placing Bibles in hotel rooms throughout the country, beginning in 1910, the Gideons have given New Testaments to many servicemen during the two World Wars. Their expanded program aims to present each school child in America with copies of the Psalms and New Testament, a practice which immediately brings up the question of sectarian influence in the schools. In Detroit, Boston, and other cities objection has been raised by Catholic or Jewish groups.[2] Many communities permit the Gideons to distribute the Scriptures to students, usually requiring a statement from the parents that it would not be objectionable to them. In Atlanta, "Members of the Gideon Bible Society are permitted by the Superintendent and Board of Education to go into the schools and give Bibles to children."[3] The practice is regulated by public opinion in many localities and if vigorous opposition develops the Gideons usually withdraw their offer. How great a religious influence results from the Gideon Bible program in the schools cannot be estimated. The mere fact that the school allows Bibles to be distributed might give added sanction to the importance of Bible study.

The survey results show that the practice of permitting the Gideons to distribute Bibles to school children is rather widespread with smaller towns allowing this activity more often than large cities. While the national average is 42.74%, the difference between the low in the East (26.24%) and the high in the South (54.77%) was large. Of the schools which permit Gideon Bibles to be given, the great majority (94.81%) use school property for the distribution.

The declining popularity of this practice is evident, the survey showing its discontinuance within the last five years by nearly one-fourth of the school systems replying to the questionnaire. Approximately one-fourth of the school systems have experienced a protest over this distribution. An interesting point shows the small amount of objection raised in the South (8.96%) over Gideon Bibles. The larger cities experience a great deal of protest (62.50%) while it is relatively uncommon (16.57%) in small towns. Despite the controversy most schools (90.95) do not plan to change existing policy.

Bus Service For Religious Schools. Public bus transportation for parochial school students is furnished in 19.86% of the communities in America. Regional differences are at once apparent: East engages in this practice in 37.96% of the localities while the South provides such service in only 3.59% of its towns and cities.

Public School Classes in Churches. Public school classes are usually not held in church buildings, according to the answers received from the survey. The national average of 7.76% indicated little adherence to such a practice. No significant deviations from this pattern can be noticed except in large cities where 22% of the respondents reported such a situation.

Religious Orders in Public Schools. Members of religious orders teach in 5.76% of American public schools. The South shows the largest percentage (9.04%) and the East the smallest (3.99%). Where this situation exists, the members of these religious orders are dressed in distinctive garb during teaching hours in about one case in five. The East, however, reports a figure of 45.83% of the school systems in which this practice was allowed.

The results of the survey relating to religious groups and public education, confirm that the "wall of separation" still stands although somewhat the worse for wear. Gideon Bibles are given to children on school property in a great many localities and public busses are being rather widely used to bring pupils to parochial school. At present, the findings indicate that neither the holding of public school classes in church buildings nor the teaching by religious orders in tax-supported institutions constitutes a significant religious influence.

CHART XVI

Are Gideon Bibles distributed in your school system?

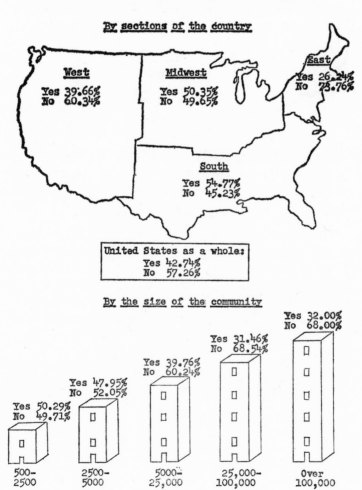

By sections of the country

West
Yes 39.66%
No 60.34%

Midwest
Yes 50.35%
No 49.65%

East
Yes 26.24%
No 73.76%

South
Yes 54.77%
No 45.23%

United States as a whole:
Yes 42.74%
No 57.26%

By the size of the community

Yes 50.29%
No 49.71%
500–2500

Yes 47.95%
No 52.05%
2500–5000

Yes 39.76%
No 60.24%
5000–25,000

Yes 31.46%
No 68.54%
25,000–100,000

Yes 32.00%
No 68.00%
Over 100,000

CHART XVII

If Gideon Bibles are distributed in schools of your system—
is this done on school property?

By sections of the country

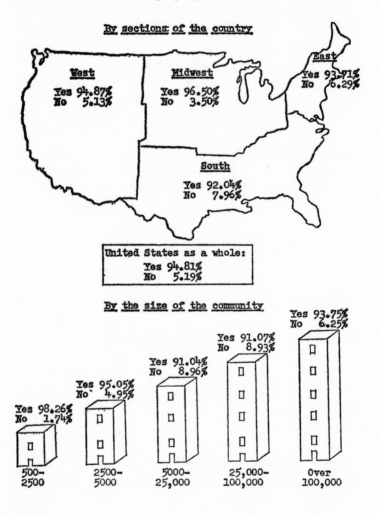

East
Yes 93.71%
No 6.29%

West
Yes 94.87%
No 5.13%

Midwest
Yes 96.50%
No 3.50%

South
Yes 92.04%
No 7.96%

United States as a whole:
Yes 94.81%
No 5.19%

By the size of the community

Yes 98.26%
No 1.74%

Yes 95.05%
No 4.95%

Yes 91.04%
No 8.96%

Yes 91.07%
No 8.93%

Yes 93.75%
No 6.25%

| 500–2500 | 2500–5000 | 5000–25,000 | 25,000–100,000 | Over 100,000 |

86

CHART XVIII

If Gideon Bibles are distributed in your school system, has there been protest about the practice?

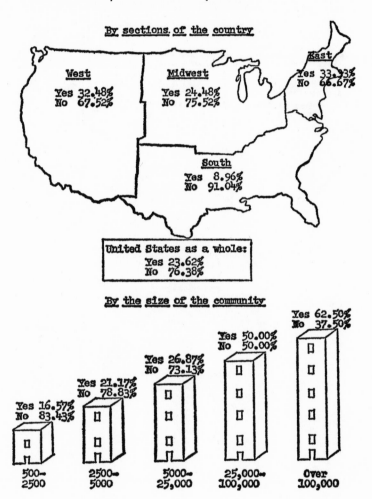

By sections of the country

East
Yes 33.33%
No 66.67%

West
Yes 32.48%
No 67.52%

Midwest
Yes 24.48%
No 75.52%

South
Yes 8.96%
No 91.04%

United States as a whole:
Yes 23.62%
No 76.38%

By the size of the community

Yes 62.50%
No 37.50%

Yes 50.00%
No 50.00%

Yes 26.87%
No 73.13%

Yes 21.17%
No 78.83%

Yes 16.57%
No 83.43%

500– 2500	2500– 5000	5000– 25,000	25,000– 100,000	Over 100,000

CHART XIX

Does your school system provide bus transportation for students attending parochial schools?

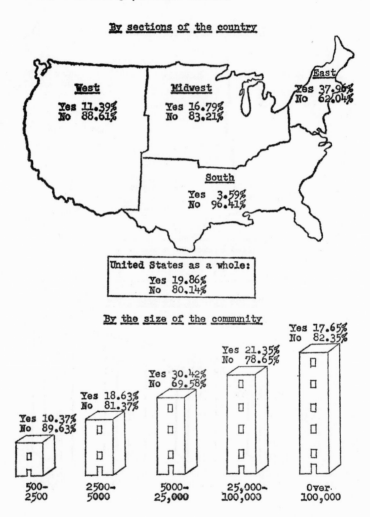

By sections of the country

West
Yes 11.39%
No 88.61%

Midwest
Yes 16.79%
No 83.21%

East
Yes 37.96%
No 62.04%

South
Yes 3.59%
No 96.41%

United States as a whole:
Yes 19.86%
No 80.14%

By the size of the community

Yes 10.37%
No 89.63%

Yes 18.63%
No 81.37%

Yes 30.42%
No 69.58%

Yes 21.35%
No 78.65%

Yes 17.65%
No 82.35%

500–
2500

2500–
5000

5000–
25,000

25,000–
100,000

Over
100,000

CHART XX

In your school system are any public school classes held in
church buildings?

By sections of the country

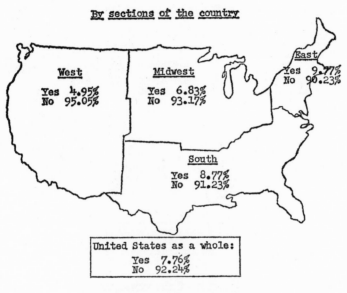

East
Yes 9.77%
No 90.23%

West
Yes 4.95%
No 95.05%

Midwest
Yes 6.83%
No 93.17%

South
Yes 8.77%
No 91.23%

United States as a whole:
Yes 7.76%
No 92.24%

By the size of the community

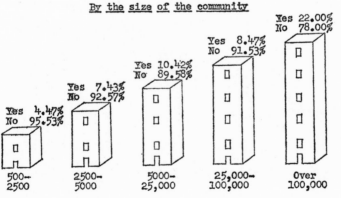

Yes 4.47%
No 95.53%

Yes 7.43%
No 92.57%

Yes 10.42%
No 89.58%

Yes 8.47%
No 91.53%

Yes 22.00%
No 78.00%

| 500–2500 | 2500–5000 | 5000–25,000 | 25,000–100,000 | Over 100,000 |

CHART XXI

Are there any members of religious orders teaching in the public schools of your system?

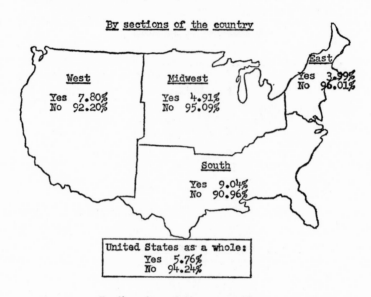

By sections of the country

East
Yes 3.99%
No 96.01%

West
Yes 7.80%
No 92.20%

Midwest
Yes 4.91%
No 95.09%

South
Yes 9.04%
No 90.96%

United States as a whole:
Yes 5.76%
No 94.24%

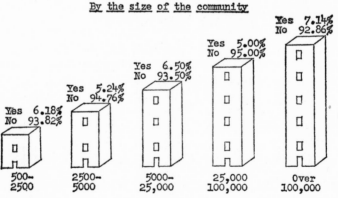

By the size of the community

Yes 6.18%
No 93.82%

Yes 5.24%
No 94.76%

Yes 6.50%
No 93.50%

Yes 5.00%
No 95.00%

Yes 7.14%
No 92.86%

| 500-2500 | 2500-5000 | 5000-25,000 | 25,000-100,000 | Over 100,000 |

CHAPTER VIII

THE SCHOOL ADMINISTRATOR SPEAKS

The shaping of school policy and curriculum in matters of religious influence, often becomes a controversial procedure. Various community forces, each one involving complex relationships, govern how much religion is allowed in the public schools. The result is tremendous diversity throughout school systems. School policy is usually determined by the following conditions or persons:

1. State Law: Inasmuch as the states have the power to educate, most of the laws regulating education are state laws. Federal laws covering freedom of religion cannot, of course, be violated by any state code.

2. Community Opinion: In some ways this is the most important factor of all for if school policy is opposed by the constituents, a change in the school board can be made through the ballot box. Localities with a variety of religious beliefs understandably have difficulty reaching consensus on the proper place of religion in the schools. On the other hand, where one faith predominates, its influence is likely to be found to a greater degree.

3. Public School Teacher: These instructors implement any policy set up to handle religion. Their attitudes and the quality of their own education for dealing with religious matters can literally make or break any school program.

4. Superintendent of Schools: The most important single person involved in policy making for a school system is the superintendent. It is therefore worthwhile to know his opinion on several controversial issues as he is in a position to either encourage or discourage any number of practices which have had been discussed in this book.

The survey questionnaire was therefore directed to him. In most cases these officials took time to personally fill in the information requested although in a few cases the task was delegated to principals or curriculum directors.

The questions asked of superintendents were somewhat "open-ended" leaving room for comment on the issues. Many administrators did expand their opinions and a few typical statements are included after the analysis of each question.

CHART XXII

What is your opinion of released time religious instruction?
(Question to school administrators)

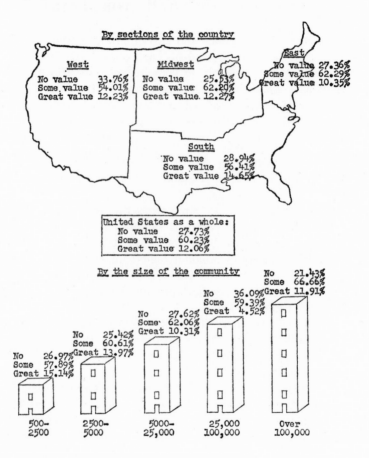

By sections of the country

West
No value   33.76%
Some value   54.01%
Great value   12.23%

Midwest
No value   25.53%
Some value   62.20%
Great value. 12.27%

East
No value 27.36%
Some value 62.29%
Great value 10.35%

South
No value   28.94%
Some value   56.41%
Great value   14.65%

United States as a whole:
No value   27.73%
Some value   60.23%
Great value   12.06%

By the size of the community

No   21.43%
Some 66.66%
Great 11.91%

No   36.09%
Some 59.39%
Great 4.52%

No   27.62%
Some 62.06%
Great 10.31%

No   25.42%
Some 60.61%
Great 13.97%

No   26.97%
Some 57.89%
Great 15.14%

500-   2500-   5000-   25,000   Over
2500   5000   25,000   100,000   100,000

92

Released Time Instruction. Released time religious education appears to be a waste of time to over one-fourth of the school officials. It has "some value" to 60.23% and "great value" to 12.06%. This pattern of opinion holds true for all sections of the country and population categories. The one exception is the small cities: only 4.52% of these communities felt that released time has "great value."

Sample comments from school administrators replying to the question "Do you favor released time instruction?" :

"Yes, it develops good habits."
"No, it is contrary to separation of church and state."
"No, time should be used for school work only."
"No, I believe it to be harmful—promoting disharmony and divisiveness."
"No, this is the task of the church outside of school hours."
"Yes, we have too little religion so it has merit."
"No, poor programs, poor instructors."
"No, I believe there is time for this after school, before school or on weekends."
"Yes, I believe it has great value—more is needed."
"Yes, it has some value but it is not the answer to real spiritual growth."
"Yes, spiritual side must not be neglected."

Religious Celebrations in School. A majority of school administrators (61.96%) feel that religious holidays can be celebrated through school activities if care is employed not to offend those of differing religious belief. A minority of 14.46% believe these types of activities to be improper while 23.58% feel the school has the right to celebrate the holidays in such ways. It is interesting that in 29.92% of the localities in the South the administrators believe the school has the right to celebrate religious holidays. Only 8.59% of Southern communities consider it improper.

Sample comments from school administrators replying to the question "Do you favor the celebration of religious holidays by school activities?"

"Yes, the education of the whole child requires holiday observances."
"Yes, should set a good example in every possible way."
"Yes, though those who do not approve should be excused."
"No, it is not legal."

What is your opinion regarding the celebration of religious holidays by school activities? (Question to school administrators)

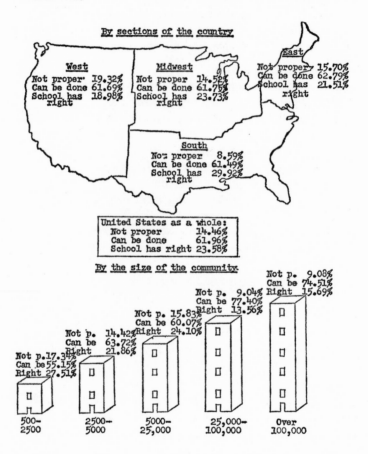

By sections of the country

West
Not proper 19.32%
Can be done 61.69%
School has 18.98%
      right

Midwest
Not proper 14.52%
Can be done 61.75%
School has 23.73%
      right

East
Not proper 15.70%
Can be done 62.79%
School has 21.51%
      right

South
Not proper 8.59%
Can be done 61.49%
School has 29.92%
      right

United States as a whole:
Not proper   14.46%
Can be done   61.96%
School has right   23.58%

By the size of the community

Not p. 17.34%
Can be 55.15%
Right 27.51%

Not p. 14.42%
Can be 63.72%
Right 21.86%

Not p. 15.83%
Can be 60.07%
Right 24.10%

Not p. 9.04%
Can be 77.40%
Right 13.56%

Not p. 9.08%
Can be 74.51%
Right 15.69%

| 500–2500 | 2500–5000 | 5000–25,000 | 25,000–100,000 | Over 100,000 |

CHART XXIV

Do you favor the distribution of Gideon Bibles in the public schools? (Question to school administrators)

By sections of the country

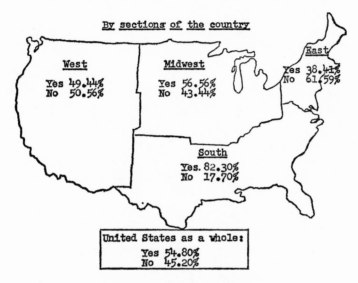

West
Yes 49.44%
No 50.56%

Midwest
Yes 56.56%
No 43.44%

East
Yes 38.41%
No 61.59%

South
Yes. 82.30%
No 17.70%

United States as a whole:
Yes 54.80%
No 45.20%

By the size of the community

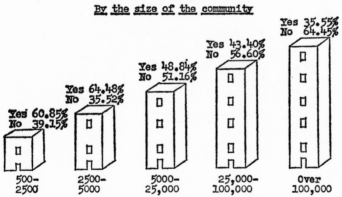

Yes 60.85%
No 39.15%

Yes 64.48%
No 35.52%

Yes 48.84%
No 51.16%

Yes 43.40%
No 56.60%

Yes 35.55%
No 64.45%

500–2500   2500–5000   5000–25,000   25,000–100,000   Over 100,000

95

"No, it is not proper unless all are celebrated and this causes many disruptions in school program."

"Yes, Christmas and Thanksgiving have become nationally accepted, others have not."

"Yes, such observances can help teach basic understandings and appreciations of various beliefs."

"Yes, school has right to celebrate if holidays are proclaimed by someone in authority (i.e. the President and Thanksgiving)."

"No, not the duty of the schools."

Gideon Bibles. More than one-half (54.80%) of school officers view the distribution of Gideon Bibles in the public schools with favor. Sectional differences are pronounced, however, and vary from a favorable response of 38.41% in the East to 82.30% in the South. Community size has a direct relationship to attitude, a high favorable reply from smaller towns contrasting with the low of large cities.

Sample comments from school administrators replying to the questions. "Do you favor the distribution of Gideon Bibles in the public schools?" :

"No, opens the door for distribution of any religious materials."

"Yes, only to those who do not have a Bible."

"Yes, no objection if school cannot or will not provide them."

"Yes, it is the only way some people can get a Bible."

"No, Bibles can be obtained by other means."

"Yes, can't do harm and might do much good."

"No, should be done through churches."

"No, not in favor unless Catholic versions are also distributed."

"Yes, I would appreciate some now for distribution to classes."

"Yes, make it strictly optional—I would prefer the school personnel make distribution."

Baccalaureate Exercises. The Baccalaureate service receives substantial and widespread support from school administrators. The national figure shows 89.26% in favor with the East giving the most reserved endorsement—76.84%.

Sample comments from school administrators replying to question: "Do you favor the Baccalaureate service in connection with high school graduation?" :

"Yes, where feasible; should be at individual churches."

"No, not necessary—carryover from church operation of schools."

"Yes, all occasions to impart spiritual truths should be utilized."
"Yes, graduation services are not complete without it."
"Yes, practiced so long that discontinuance would be protested."
"Yes, students don't know enough about God and His Program."
"We merely follow custom. I'm rather neutral on the idea."
"No. Illegal. Ours are not called Baccalaureate and are held in two churches, one Protestant and one Roman Catholic."

Fringe Benefits. The use of public tax money for the so-called "fringe benefits" for parochial schools was looked upon with disfavor by the large majority of school officials (86.25%).

Sample comments from school administrators replying to the question: "Do you favor using public tax money for "fringe benefits" for parochial school children (transportation, textbooks, etc.)?" :

"No, not enough money for both parochial and public schools."
"Never!"
"Yes, parochial school buildings and teachers take burden off public schools."
"Yes, parents of parochial school students all paying taxes and should have benefits."
"No, would be the downfall of American public education."
"No, private schools should be self-sufficient."
"Transportation yes—textbooks no."
"Yes, we do not differentiate for other social services, i.e. police, fire, water, etc. Why select education as the one public service to be handled differently?"
"No, fringe benefits are benefits. I do not believe any public funds should go to private schools for any purpose."

Treatment of Religion in Schools. The final question of the survey deals with the adequacy with which religion is handled in the various school systems. Most of the administrators (77.47%) feel that it is being treated in a reasonably sound manner. There is very small fluctuation from this opinion in the four sections of the country or in the five divisions of community size.

Sample comments from school administrators replying to the question: "Do you believe your school system is dealing in an adequate way with religion?" :

"No, I am not satisfied."
"No, should be more Bible taught."

CHART XXV

Do you favor Baccalaureate services in connection with high school graduation? (Question to school administrators)

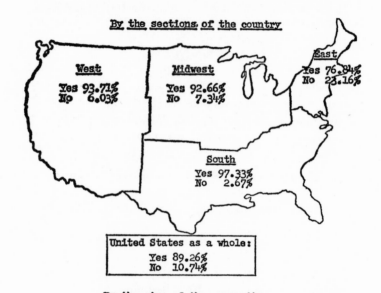

By the sections of the country

West
Yes 93.71%
No 6.03%

Midwest
Yes 92.66%
No 7.34%

East
Yes 76.84%
No 23.16%

South
Yes 97.33%
No 2.67%

United States as a whole:
Yes 89.26%
No 10.74%

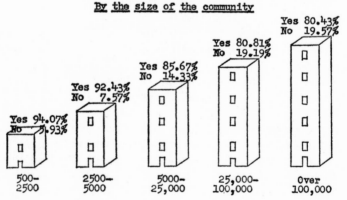

By the size of the community

Yes 94.07%
No 5.93%

Yes 92.43%
No 7.57%

Yes 85.67%
No 14.33%

Yes 80.81%
No 19.19%

Yes 80.43%
No 19.57%

500–2500

2500–5000

5000–25,000

25,000–100,000

Over 100,000

CHART XXVI

Do you favor the use of public tax money for "fringe benefits" for parochial school children—i.e. transportation, textbooks, etc.? (Question to school administrators)

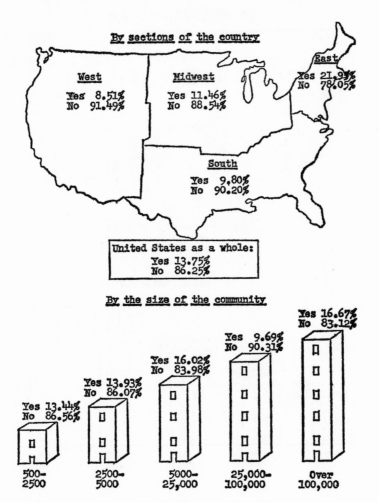

By sections of the country

West
Yes 8.51%
No 91.49%

Midwest
Yes 11.46%
No 88.54%

East
Yes 21.9%
No 78.05%

South
Yes 9.80%
No 90.20%

United States as a whole:
Yes 13.75%
No 86.25%

By the size of the community

Yes 13.44%
No 86.56%

Yes 13.93%
No 86.07%

Yes 16.02%
No 83.98%

Yes 9.69%
No 90.31%

Yes 16.67%
No 83.12%

500–2500

2500–5000

5000–25,000

25,000–100,000

Over 100,000

99

CHART XXVII

Do you believe your school system is dealing in an adequate
way with religion? (Question to school administrators)

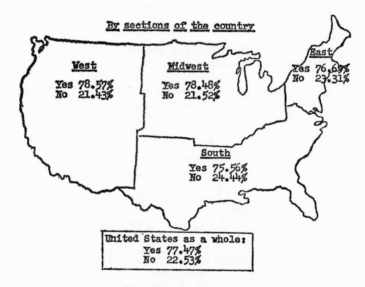

By sections of the country

West
Yes 78.57%
No 21.43%

Midwest
Yes 78.48%
No 21.52%

East
Yes 76.69%
No 23.31%

South
Yes 75.56%
No 24.44%

United States as a whole:
Yes 77.47%
No 22.53%

By the size of the community

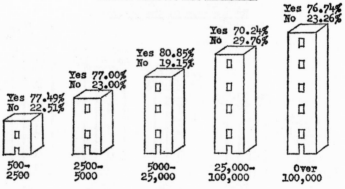

Yes 77.49%
No 22.51%

Yes 77.00%
No 23.00%

Yes 80.85%
No 19.15%

Yes 70.24%
No 29.76%

Yes 76.74%
No 23.26%

500-
2500

2500-
5000

5000-
25,000

25,000-
100,000

Over
100,000

"Yes, church and state should be separate."

"No, should do more to emphasize Christian principles."

"Yes, religious teaching is the responsibility and privilege of the home and church not the public schools."

"Yes, by ignoring it!"

"Only the Lord knows."

"No, I believe courses in religion can and should be offered to all those who wish to elect them."

"Yes, we are not a church or a home. There is not enough school time for school work."

In summary, school superintendents look with reservation on released time programs, the majority feeling they have some value but twice as many being opposed as in favor of them. They view the celebration of religious holidays by school activities with caution, a majority believing it can be done if care is exercised not to offend the religious convictions of those of different persuasions. The superintendents are rather divided on the distribution of Gideon Bibles in the public schools although a small majority advocate the practice.

They favor the Baccalaureate service as a part of high school graduation, and oppose the use of public tax funds for "fringe benefits" for parochial school students.

On the whole they are satisfied that their school systems are handling religion in an adequate way.

CHAPTER IX

THE OVERALL PICTURE

The Apostle Paul expressed the sentiments of the writer when he exclaimed, "And what shall I more say? Time would fail me . . ."

It is unnecessary to belabor the extent and complexity of a subject whose basic issues involve constitutional freedoms, religious conviction, and the education of youth. Emotional overtones are inescapable in matters which touch on religious belief. Strong feelings arise within adherents of one point of view or another, and emotion often overwhelms reason in dealing with the problems that arise.

A great number of small and perhaps inconsequential generalizations could be made. However, to avoid this pitfall only items of major worth will be included. The central points will be presented not as final and absolute, but as reasonable assumptions based on evidence. The following conclusions seem warranted:

Great Interest in the Problem. With the revival of interest in religion throughout America, the place of religion in public education becomes a great concern to laymen, educators, and clergymen. Church bodies have drafted statements and resolutions on the subject and professional education groups have conducted studies on ways and means of dealing with religion in the public schools. If interest remains at the present high, continued controversy will involve educational institutions at all levels.

American Tradition on the Subject Varies. There is no single "American tradition" in the handling of religion in the schools. Early colonial schools were religiously dominated with Christian teachings forming a large part of the curriculum. As the public school movement spread during the early part of the nineteenth century, the Bible and nondenominational religious instruction played important roles in education. State and federal laws, together with pressure from competing denominations, gradually eliminated most of the religious content of the public school curriculum. By 1900 the schools were largely secular, a condition which has extended to the present time. Those who advocate more religion in our schools can point to one period as the "American tradition," while opponents cite another period to support their views. The federal Constitution is sufficiently vague to allow both sides to quote it to reinforce their arguments. The wisdom of basing contemporary policy on practices used in our country a hundred or two hundred years ago can be questioned. The nature of modern American culture and society is different enough from times past to encourage new approaches to our problems. If a solution is pursued with due regard to lessons learned from experience, but without being chained to tradition, acceptable patterns of action will more quickly be worked out.

The Rights of Parochial Schools Emphasized. Parochial schools have been given the judicial right to exist through Supreme Court decision (Pierce v. Society of Sisters) and in certain instances the right to tax money for some aspects of their operation. The privilege of parents to educate their children in religious schools has been firmly recognized.

Wide Diversity Found in State Laws on Religion and Education. A great lack of uniformity exists in state laws regarding religion in public education. The federal Constitution, which does not deal with education, enforces through its First and Fourteenth Amendments, religious liberty and the separation of church and state. While these freedoms are guaranteed by every state constitution, the legal status of religion in the schools of each state varies greatly.

Judicial Decisions Show Differing Views. Both state and federal courts have interpreted the meaning of laws dealing with religion and education with widely divergent opinions. Even the United States Supreme Court has reversed itself on cases dealing with freedom of religion. It appears clear that no single interpretation of the meaning of religious liberty and separation of church and state can be found in court decisions on either the state or federal level.

School Systems Vary in Religious Emphasis. The emphasis placed on religion in individual school systems throughout the nation differs greatly. In a number of localities even the facts of religious heritage are eliminated for fear of controversy, while in others not only are students taught "about religion" but moral and spiritual values are based on religious sanctions. Actual practices follow a continuum from carefully avoiding all religiously tinged topics to compulsory Bible reading, class devotionals, prayers, and denominational teaching on public school premises.

The Place of Religion Depends on Several Factors. The type of relationship between religion and any public system of education is determined by local community opinion, desires of school officials, attitudes and training of the teachers, and state and national laws bearing on the subject.

Sectarian Bodies Push Their Viewpoints. Denominational church groups are exerting pressure on school officials for the inclusion of more religion in the public schools. Most of this influence comes from Protestant bodies while much of the opposition arises from Jewish groups. A number of Protestant churches have adopted, through their official governing bodies, statements urging the schools to do more in emphasizing religion.

Curricular Activities and Religion. The formal course offerings of American schools often contain items of religious emphasis. The aims of instruction include not only moral but spiritual values. Teachers receive material to help them in handling moral and spiritual aspects as well as the factual teaching about the historical and cultural impact of religion. Bible reading is popular in Eastern and Southern areas but not in Midwestern or Western parts of the country. Sectional differences are also pronounced in other curricular practices involving religion.

Religious Influence Through Non-curricular Activities. The public schools of the United States provide a number of activities outside the regular curriculum which contain elements of religion. The following practices are found in a large majority of systems:

1. Baccalaureate services
2. School activities in celebration of Thanksgiving, Christmas, and Easter.
3. Excusing students to attend special holy day services.

Other customs are found in varying degrees of popularity depending on community conditions.

Released Time Increases Gradually. Released time religious instruction appears to be growing slowly but as yet does not seem a satisfactory solution to the problem.

Schools and Sectarian Groups. Public school systems have little official contact with religious groups with the exception of the Gideon Society. This group distributes Bibles in about two-fifths of the schools. In approximately one-fifth of the localities public school busses are used for parochial schools.

Superintendents View Situation. The administrators of America's public school systems generally look with favor upon the following practices:

1. Celebration of religious holidays in public schools.
2. Distribution of Gideon Bibles in public schools.
3. Baccalaureate services.

They are cautious about endorsing the released time program of religious instruction. These officials roundly condemn use of tax money to provide so-called "fringe benefits" to parochial schools. They also feel satisfied that religion is being handled in an adequate way.

Similarity of Treatment. The information brought out by the study indicates that many school systems are alike in the way they handle certain aspects of religion. This extends not only to sectional areas but population categories as well. A few illustrations bring out this fact:

1. Public school classes are not commonly held in church buildings to a large extent in any section of the country.
2. Teachers in all parts of the country are provided with materials to help in teaching about religion.
3. Religious holidays are celebrated through school activities across the nation with only small sectional differences.

Sectional Differences Pronounced. This issue, however, is a two-sided coin with one surface showing uniformity while the other demonstrates variety in treatment. Marked differences appear more apparent, however, than similarities. Some examples point out this diversity:

1. Bible reading is popular in the East and South, but not in the West or Midwest.
2. Gideon Bibles are distributed in over one-half the schools in the Midwest and South but only one-fourth of those in the East.
3. Public bus transportation to parochial schools is furnished in over

a third of the communities in the East but in much smaller percentages in the West, Midwest, and South.

More Religion in Southern Schools. Religious influence appears to play a larger part in the schools of the South than in any other section. While this situation does not show up in every area of the study, it is so pronounced that the conclusion is inescapable. A few cases will help to prove the contention:

1. A larger percentage of the schools of the South teach spiritual values than in other sections of the country.

2. Regular chapel exercises are much more popular in the schools of the region than in the East, Midwest, or West.

3. The South likewise leads the other areas of the nation in Bible reading in its schools.

Relation Between Religion and Population Category Not Great. The size of the community does not seem to indicate how religion will be treated in the school system. Illustrations of this can be found by looking through the tables and charts of this report. The larger cities at first glance appear to permit more religious influence than other size categories, but a closer look will reveal situations of a directly reverse nature.

American Public Schools Do Not Eliminate All Religious Influence. The public schools of the United States cannot be said to be Godless or secular upon the basis of the information in this survey. Many critics have blasted public education for this supposed lack, but the figures here put the lie to the charge. A number of illustrations in this report buttress the argument that the majority of school systems:

1. Teach spiritual values.

2. Provide material to teachers to help in teaching *about* religion.

3. Conduct baccalaureate services in connection with graduation.

4. Observe religious holidays through school programs.

Some Practices May Be Illegal. A number of activities employed in some school systems might be questioned in the light of previous court decisions. While it can never be predicted which way a legal ruling will go, several activities, such as the following, could border on the unlawful:

1. Released time classes which are held on school property. This is especially true in the South where over half such classes were conducted on public premises. The McCollum decision by the U.S. Supreme Court called this practice a breach of the Constitution.

2. Regular classes in the Bible taught by teachers paid by public funds might be held a violation of separation of church and state.

3. The legality of the distribution of Gideon Bibles might be challenged in the light of an adverse decision in New Jersey.

It is possible that many of the activities described by this investigation would be found contrary to the law if protest about them were made. A court case requires money, time, and interest, however, and often one or more of these elements is missing.

*   *   *

It is not the purpose of this book to pass judgment on the correctness or legality of the practices which are reported but rather to gather information which indicates the influence of religion in American public schools. Through a more factual knowledge of the present situation, it is hoped that a greater understanding of the problems and issues involved will be gained.

Interest, controversy and experimentation seem to characterize the present relationship between religion and public education in the United States. The interest is understandably general, a great majority of American children being educated in our public schools; it is also increasingly specific as current religious animation arouses forces which demand more emphasis on religion in public schools.

The controversy is rooted in America's religious heterogeneity and in efforts to reach solutions that satisfy the majority of the people involved. Unfortunately, at the same time, these efforts incite denominational jealousy in viewing programs of religion in the schools, with additional disagreement resulting from varying interpretations of the laws separating church and state. The experimentation is an effort by public educators and laymen of all ranks to devise sound approaches to the requests of religious groups without violating the laws establishing freedom of religion and separation of church and state. On this monumental task immense energy, consummate skill, and enormous understanding must be concentrated. Only through efforts of gargantuan dimensions will this complex and baffling problem be resolved so that God and Caesar may truly assume proportions commensurate with the sentiments of the American people.

REFERENCES

CHAPTER I

1. *New York Times,* July 15, 1961.
2. *Minneapolis Sunday Tribune,* January 8, 1961.
3. *St. Paul Dispatch,* September 8, 1961.
4. Details about the procedures used in the survey are available from the author.
5. Reinhold Neibuhr, "Varieties of Religious Revival," *The New Republic,* June 6, 1955, p. 13.
6. *Religion and the Public School* (New York: Joint Advisory Committee, 1956), p. 5.
7. *Ibid.,* p. 10.
8. *Bulletin of the National Catholic Education Association,* Vol. 51, No. 1 (August, 1954), p. 39.
9. *Ibid.,* p. 49.
10. "The Relation of Religion to Public Education" (Committee on Religion and Public Education of the National Council of Churches in the U.S.A.), *International Journal of Religious Education,* April, 1960, p. 32.
11. *Discipline of the Methodist Church,* 1952 (duplicated by the National Council of the Churches of Christ in the U.S.A., Chicago, March 3, 1953), p. 652.

CHAPTER II

1. John Russell Bartlett (ed.), *Records of the Colony of Rhode Island and Providence Plantation in New England* (Providence, Rhode Island: Knowles and Anthony, State Printers, 1859), Vol. IV, 206.
2. R. Freeman Butts and Lawrence A. Cremin, *A History of Education in American Culture* (New York: Henry Holt and Co., 1953), p. 69.
3. H. S. Commager, *Documents of American History* (3rd ed.; New York: F. S. Crofts, 1947), p. 29.
4. Herbert L. Osgood, *The American Colonies in the Seventeenth Century* (New York: Macmillan Co., 1904), Vol. II, pp. 335-36.
5. F. N. Thorpe, *The Federal and State Constitutions, Colonial Charters and Other Organic Laws* (Washington, D.C.: Government Printing Office, 1909), p. 3255.
6. Leo Pfeffer, *Freedom of Religion and Separation of Church and State* (mimeographed; New York: American Jewish Congress, 1955), p. 7.
7. *Ibid.,* p. 8.
8. *Ibid.,* p. 8.
9. *Ibid.,* p. 14.
10. Leo Pfeffer, *Church, State, and Freedom* (Boston: Beacon Press, 1953), p. 282.
11. Raymond B. Culver, *Horace Mann and Religion in the Massachusetts Public Schools* (New Haven, Connecticut: Yale University Press, 1929), p. 207.
12. Horace Mann, *Twelfth Annual Report of the Board of Education* (Boston: Dutton and Wentworth, State Printers, 1849) pp. 104-5.

13. *New York Freeman's Journal,* Vol. 1, No. 2 (July 11, 1840), p. 12.

14. Matthew Hale Smith, *The Bible, The Rod, and Religion in Common Schools* (Boston: Wm. B. Fowle, 1846), p. 11.

15. Frederick E. Ellis (ed.), "Parochial and Public Schools," *The Educational Forum,* Vol. 14 (1949), p. 21. Dr. Ellis has translated a number of the pronouncements of the Third Plenary Council of Baltimore from their original Latin into English. These pronouncements relative to parochial and public education are included in *The Educational Forum,* Vol. 14 (1949), pp. 25-37.

16. *Five Great Encyclicals* (New York: The Paulist Press, 1949), pp. 39-55.

17. "Unification and Education," *Catholic World,* Vol. 13 (1871), pp. 1-14.

18. R. Freeman Butts, *The American Tradition in Religion and Education* (Boston: Beacon Press, 1950), p. 144.

19. *Ibid.,* p. 145.

CHAPTER III

1. Henry Steele Commager, editor, "The Northwest Ordinance," *Documents of American History* (New York: F. S. Crofts and Co., 1934), p. 130.

2. Anson Phelps Stokes, *Church and State in the United States* (New York: Harper and Brothers, 1950), Vol. III, p. 443.

3. A. W. Johnson and F. H. Yost, *The Separation of Church and State in the United States* (Minneapolis, Minnesota: University of Minnesota Press, 1948), pp. 9-10.

4. R. Freeman Butts, *The American Tradition in Religion and Education* (Boston: Beacon Press, 1950), pp. 92-94.

5. Saul K. Padover, *The Complete Jefferson* (New York: Duell Sloan and Pearce, 1943), pp. 518-19.

6. Meyer v. Nebraska 262 U.S. 390 (1923).

7. Following are listed the states and the article and section which contain the guarantee of religious freedom, the Article in Roman numerals and the section in Arabic numbers. (Alabama I, 3), (Arizona II, 12), (Arkansas II, 24), (California I, 4), (Colorado II, 4), (Connecticut I, 3 and 4), (Delaware I, 1), (Florida Declaration of Rights, 5 and 6), (Georgia I, 13 and 14), (Idaho I, 4), (Illinois II, 3), (Indiana I, 2, 2, and 4), (Iowa I, 3), (Kansas, Bill of Rights, 7), (Kentucky Bill of Rights, 5), (Louisiana I, 4), (Maine I, 3), (Maryland Declaration of Rights, 36), (Massachusetts Amendment XI), (Michigan II, 3), (Minnesota I, 16), (Mississippi III, 18), (Missouri II, 5 and 7), (Montana III, 4), (Nebraska I, 4), (Nevada I, 4), (New Hampshire Bill of Rights 5 and 6), (New Jersey I, 3), (New Mexico II, 11), (New York I, 3), (North Carolina I, 26, (North Dakota I, 4), (Ohio I, 7), (Oklahoma I, 2,), (Oregon I, 2, 3, and 5), (Pennsylvania I, 3), (Rhode Island I, 3), (South Carolina I, 4), (South Dakota VI, 3), (Tennessee I, 3), (Texas I, 6), (Utah I, 4), (Vermont I, 3), (Virginia I, 16), (Washington I, 11), (West Virginia III, 15), (Wisconsin I, 18), (Wyoming I, 18) as found in: New York State Constitutional Convention Committee, *Constitutions of the States of the United States* (Albany, 1938), *passim.*

8. Constitution of the State of New Hampshire as found in New York State Constitutional Convention Committee, *Constitutions of the States of the United States* (Albany, 1938), p. 1034.

9. Constitution of the State of Vermont, p. 1566.

10. Don Conway, "Religion and Public Education in the States," *International Journal of Religious Education*, March, 1956, pp. 34-40.

11. Pennsylvania's Bible reading statute has been changed to allow students who do not wish to remain in the classroom to leave during the actual reading.

12. *State of Maine Laws Relating to Public Schools* (Augusta, Maine: State Department of Education, 1955), p. 51.

13. *School Laws of Iowa* (Section 9, Chapter 280; Des Moines: State of Iowa Department of Public Instruction, 1954), p. 199.

14. *1956 State Code* (Section 251, Article 22, Chapter 4; Carson City, Nevada: State Printing Office).

15. The Oregon Supreme Court ruled late in 1961 that providing free textbooks to parochial schools was unconstitutional. Dickman et. al. v. School Dist. No. 62c Oregon City, Oregon, 366 Pac. 2d 533 (1961).

16. Wisconsin should be added to this list because the Wisconsin legislature late in 1961 passed a bill allowing public school busses to transport parochial school pupils to public schools, from where they will walk to the parochial school.

17. *General School Laws, State of Michigan,* Revision of 1955 (Section 591, Chapter 9; Lansing, Michigan: State Printers, 1955), p. 118.

18. *School Laws of Iowa,* Iowa State Code (Section 5, Chapter 285; Des Moines, Iowa: State of Iowa Department of Public Instruction, 1954), p. 221.

19. *School Laws of Pennsylvania 1953,* Constitution of 1873, Commonwealth of Pennsylvania (Section 17, Article 3; Harrisburg, Pennsylvania: Department of Public Instruction, 1953), p. 2.

20. R. H. Noll, *The School Laws of South Dakota 1955* (Section 3202, Chapter 15; Sioux Falls, South Dakota: Midwest Beach Co., 1955), p. 173.

21. *Missouri School Laws 1956* (Section 10, Chapter 166; Jefferson City, Missouri: State Department of Education, 1956), pp. 161-62.

22. Alton B. Jones (ed.), "School Laws of the State of Idaho, *Idaho Bulletin of Education,* (Vol. 35, No. 1, Section 6, Article 9; Boise, Idaho, 1949), p. 20.

23. *Nebraska School Laws 1955-6* (Section 79-1274, Article 12; Lincoln, Nebraska: Stephenson School Supply Co., 1956), p. 241.

24. Pierce v. Society of Sisters, 268 U.S. 510 (1924).

25. *Ibid.*

26. Cochran v. Board of Education, 281 U.S. 370 (1930).

27. Minersville School District v. Gobitis, 310 U.S. 586 (1940).

28. Board of Education v. Barnette, 319 U.S. 624 (1943).

29. The United States Supreme Court in 1961 upheld the constitutionality of public bus transportation for parochial school children by declining to hear an appeal from a group of taxpayers in Newton, Connecticut. [Snyder v. Town of Newtown, 147 Conn. 374, 161 A. 2nd 770 (1960); *Cert. denied,* 365 U.S. 299 (1961)].

30. Everson v. Board of Education, 330 U.S. 1 (1947).

31. *Ibid.*

32. McCollum v. Board of Education, 333 U.S. 203 (1948).

33. Zorach v. Clauson, 343 U.S. 306 (1952).

34. "The State and Sectarian Education," *National Education Association Research Bulletin,* Vol. 34, No. 4 (Washington, D.C.: Research Division, National Education Association, December, 1956), p. 196.

35. Wilkerson v. City of Rome, 152 Ga. 652 (1921).

36. Carden v. Bland, 288 S.W. (2d) 722-25 (Tennessee, 1956).

37. R. Freeman Butts, *The American Tradition in Religious and Education* (Boston: Beacon Press, 1950), p. 195.

38. People v. Board of Education of District 24, 92 N.E. 251 (Illinois, 1910).

39. A recent Wisconsin law allows transportation of parochial school students to public school from where they will walk to their own schools.

40. Gurney et al. v. Ferguson et al., 122 Pac. (2d) 1002 Oklahoma (1942).

41. *Educational Law* (Albany, N.Y.: University of the State of New York), Bulletin #1345, p. 110.

42. Smith v. Donahue et al., 195 NYS 722, (1922).

43. Borden v. Louisiana State Board of Education, 123 So. 655 (1929).

44. The Oregon supreme court in 1961 overthrew a twenty-year-old Oregon law allowing school districts to furnish textbooks to parochial schools.

CHAPTER IV

1. F. Ernest Johnson, *American Education and Religion* (New York: Harper and Brothers, 1952), p. 15.

2. McCollum v. Board of Education, 333 U.S. 203 (1948).

3. Letter to the writer, May 14, 1957.

4. Board of Education of the City of New York, *The Development of Moral and Spiritual Ideals in the Public Schools* (New York, 1956), pp. 4-5.

5. "Moral and Spiritual Values in the St. Louis Public Schools," *The St. Louis Public School Journal,* Vol. 7, No. 3, (January, 1954), 19 pp.

6. Letter to the writer, April 23, 1957.

7. Regents of the University of the State of New York, *America's Moral and Spiritual Heritage* (Albany, New York: State Department of Education), 13 pp.

8. *Ibid.,* p. 6.

9. *Ibid.,* p. 12.

10. *Newsweek,* Vol. 46, No. 20, (November 14, 1955,) p. 101.

11. *New York Times,* October 5, 1956, p. 27.

12. Board of Education of the City of New York, *op. cit.,* p. 4.

13. *Ibid.,* p. 5.

14. *Ibid.,* p. 6.

15. Los Angeles City Schools, *Moral and Spiritual Values in Education,* Publication 580, (Los Angeles, 1954), 122 pp.

16. *Ibid.,* p. 1.

17. *Ibid.,* p. 2.

18. *Ibid.,* p. 3.

19. *Ibid.,* p. 5.

20. *Ibid.,* p. 11.

21. *Ibid.,* p. 13.

22. Idaho State Board of Education, *List of Selections from the Standard American Version of the Bible for Daily Reading in the Public Schools* (mimeographed; Boise, Idaho: no date), p. 1.

23. *Ibid.,* pp. 1-15.

24. Committee on Elementary Curriculum, *The Elementary Curriculum of the Meridian, Mississippi Public Schools,* 1940, pp. 4-5, reproduced by the Department of Religion and Public Education, National Council of Churches in the U.S.A. (Chicago, 1955).

25. Letter to the writer, May 16, 1957.

26. From a letter to the writer by Curtis G. Gentry, Director of Instruction, Knoxville City Schools, Knoxville, Tennessee, May 13, 1957.

27. Frank L. Williams, Assistant Superintendent of the Dallas Independent School District, "Information Concerning Bible Courses," mimeographed, no date, 1 page.

28. *Fostering Moral and Spiritual Development through School Activities,* Curriculum Bulletin No. 53CBM55, (Houston, Texas Public Schools, 1954), pp. 43-56.

29. *Rules of the Board of School Commissioners of Baltimore City* (Baltimore Public Schools, 1961), p. 95.

30. Community Teachers Association of Springfield, Missouri, "Moral and Spiritual Values in the Springfield Public Schools." Reproduced by the Department of Religion and Public Education of the National Council of Churches of Christ in the U.S.A. (Chicago, 1954), p. 2.

31. Letter to the writer from J. E. Goss, Curriculum Assistant, Tulsa Public Schools, June 19, 1957.

32. *The Richmond Times-Dispatch,* October 21, 1951, Section A, p. 1.

33. C. M. Dannelly, "Montgomery, Alabama, Devotional Practice," *The School Executive,* December, 1950, p. 61.

34. Knoxville Public Schools, *A Study of Youth and Their Needs* (Knoxville Board of Education, 1955), p. 3.

35. Indianapolis Public Schools, *Our Religious Heritage* (Indianapolis, Indiana, 1954), p. 23.

39. J. E. Goss, *op. cit.*

37. *Ibid.,* p. 7.

38. West High School, Denver, Colorado "Unit-Philosophy and Religious Values" (mimeographed, no date), p. 3.

39. J. E. Gross, *op. cit.*

40. Harold A. Pflug, "Religion in Missouri Textbooks," *Phi Delta Kappan,* Vol. 36, No. 7, (April, 1955), p. 259.

41. *Ibid.,* p. 259.

42. *Ibid.,* pp. 259-60.

43. A. P. Stokes, *Church and State in the United States,* (New York: Harper and Brothers, 1950), Vol. II, p. 582.

44. McCollum v. Board of Education, 333 U.S. 236 (1948).

45. Knoxville Public Schools, *op. cit.,* 4.

CHAPTER V

1. *Richmond Times-Dispatch,* October 21, 1951, p. 1.

2. C. C. Crawford, "New Holland Meets Special Problems," *The School Executive,* December, 1950, p. 65.

3. Board of Education, Pittsburgh, Pennsylvania, "Moral and Spiritual Values in the Pittsburgh Public Schools," *Pittsburgh Schools,* Vol. 28, No. 5 (May-June, 1954), p. 195.

4. Letter to the writer from J. E. Goss, Curriculum Assistant, Tulsa Public Schools, June 19, 1957.

5. *Ibid.*

6. Letter to the writer from Julia Clifton, Department of Research, Atlanta Public School System, Atlanta, Georgia, April 25, 1957.

7. Letter to the writer from L. E. Winter, Assistant Superintendent, Portland Public Schools, April 16, 1957.

8. *Richmond Times Dispatch, loc. cit.*

9. Letter to the writer from Arthur R. Olson, Director Division of Instructional Services, Denver Public Schools, Denver, Colorado, April 26, 1957.

10. *Richmond Times-Dispatch, loc. cit.*

11. *Fostering Moral and Spiritual Development Through School Activities,* Curriculum Bulletin No. 53CBM55 (Houston, Texas Public Schools, 1954), p. 43.

12. Don Conway, "Religion and Public Education in the State," *International Journal of Religious Education,* March, 1956, p. 37.

13. Committee on Elementary Curriculum, *The Elementary Curriculum of the Meridian, Mississippi Public Schools,* reproduced by the National Council of Churches of Christ in the U.S.A. (Chicago, 1955), p. 4.

14. *Richmond Times-Dispatch, loc. cit.*

15. Clifton, *loc. cit.*

16. Conway, *op. cit.,* p. 38.

17. *Ibid.*

18. Arthur E. Thompson, *State of North Dakota, General School Laws,* Chapter 36, Article 3, Section 579 (Department of Public Instruction, 1935), p. 223.

19. Letter to the writer from William E. Barrett, Vice President, Brigham Young University, Provo, Utah, June 27, 1927.

20. *Ibid.*

CHAPTER VI

1. James N. O'Neill, *The Catholic in Secular Education* (New York: Longmans, Green and Co., 1956), p. 107.

2. Leo Pfeffer,*Church, State and Freedom* (Boston: Beacon Press, 1953), p. 334.

3. Lutheran Church—Missouri Synod, *Report of Board of Parish Education* (Houston, Texas, 1953), p. 330.

4. General Board of Education of the Methodist Church, "Statement on Church and Public School Relations" (Nashville, Tennessee: The Methodist Church, 1956), pp. 1 and 3-4.

5. Board of Christian Education, Presbyterian Church (U.S.A.), *The Church and the Public Schools* (Philadelphia: Presbyterian Church in the U.S.A., 1957), pp. 5-7.

6. From a letter to the writer by Wm. E. Barrett, June 27, 1957.

7. Board of Christian Social Action, American Lutheran Church, "The Christian and His Public Schools" (Columbus, Ohio: 1954), American Lutheran Church, p. 4.

8. The American Jewish Committee, *Religion in Public Education: A Statement of Views* (New York, 1955), pp. 14-15; and Joint Advisory Committee, *Religion and the Public School* (New York, 1956), pp. 9-10.

9. C. L. Hay, *The Blind Spot in American Public Education* (New York: The Macmillan Co., 1950), p. 23.

10. V. T. Thayer, *The Attack upon the American Secular School* (Boston: Beacon Press, 1951), p. 199.

11. Mary D. Davis, *Week-Day Religious Instruction,* United States Office of Education, Pamphlet No. 36 (Washington, D.C.: Superintendent of Documents, Government Printing Office, 1933), p. 4.

12. Mary D. Davis, *Week-Day Religious Instruction,* United States Office of Education, Bulletin No. 3 (Washington, D.C.: Superintendent of Documents, Government Printing Office, 1941), p. 16.

13. Research Division, National Education Association, *The Status of Religious Education in the Public Schools* (Washington, D.C.: National Education Association, 1949), p. 8.

CHAPTER VII

1. Research Division, National Education Association, *The State and Sectarian Education* (Washington, D.C.: National Education Association, 1956), p. 186.

2. Leo Pfeffer, *Church, State, and Freedom* (Boston: Beacon Press, 1953), pp. 393-94.

3. Letter to the writer from Julia Clifton, Department of Research, Atlanta Public School System, Atlanta, Georgia, April 25, 1957.

MR 26 66				
JY 6 - '67				